Atlas c

Scale 1:250,000 o

C000068249

Route planner	II–III
Ferry services	II
Restricted motorway junctions	II

Map pages	**IV**

Atlas symbols	**1**

Road maps 1:250,000 scale	**2–83**
Western Isles 1:700,000 scale	84–85
Orkney Islands 1:636,000 scale	86
Shetland Islands 1:636,000 scale	87

Mileage chart	**88**

Index to place names	**89–108**
County, administrative area map	89
Place name index	90–108

3rd edition November 2015

© AA Media Limited 2015

Original edition printed 2008.

Cartography:
All cartography in this atlas edited, designed and produced by the Mapping Services Department of AA Publishing (A05374).

This atlas contains Ordnance Survey data © Crown copyright and database right 2015.

Publisher's notes:
Published by AA Publishing (a trading name of AA Media Limited, whose registered office is Fanum House, Basing View, Basingstoke, Hampshire RG21 4EA, UK.
Registered number 06112600).

ISBN: 978 0 7495 7769 8

A CIP catalogue record for this book is available from The British Library.

Disclaimer:
The contents of this atlas are believed to be correct at the time of the latest revision, it will not contain any subsequent amended, new or temporary information including diversions and traffic control or enforcement systems. The publishers cannot be held responsible or liable for any loss or damage occasioned to any person acting or refraining from action as a result of any use or reliance on material in this atlas, nor for any errors, omissions or changes in such material. This does not affect your statutory rights.

The publishers would welcome information to correct any errors or omissions and to keep this atlas up to date. Please write to the Atlas Editor, AA Publishing, The Automobile Association, Fanum House, Basing View, Basingstoke, Hampshire RG21 4EA, UK.
E-mail: *roadatlasfeedback@theaa.com*

Acknowledgements:
AA Publishing would like to thank the following for their assistance in producing this atlas:

RoadPilot mobile Information on fixed speed camera locations provided by and © 2015 RoadPilot Ltd. Crematoria data provided by the Cremation Society of Great Britain. Forestry Commission, Historic Scotland, National Trust for Scotland, RSPB, The Wildlife Trust, Scottish Natural Heritage.

Printer:
Printed in Dubai by Oriental Press.

Ferry services

Hebrides and west coast Scotland
Caledonian MacBrayne .... *calmac.co.uk*
Western Ferries *(Gourock-Dunoon)* .... *western-ferries.co.uk*

Orkney and Shetland
NorthLink Ferries
(Scrabster/Aberdeen-Orkney/Shetland Islands)...... *northlinkferries.co.uk*
Pentland Ferries
(Gills-St Margaret's Hope, South Ronaldsay).......... *pentlandferries.co.uk*
Orkney Ferries (inter-island).................................... *orkneyferries.co.uk*
Shetland Islands Council Ferries (inter-island) .... *shetland.gov.uk/ferries*

Ireland
Stena Line (Cairnryan-Belfast)................................ *stenaline.co.uk*
P&O Ferries (Cairnryan/Troon-Larne) .... *poferries.com*

Restricted motorway junctions

M8 Edinburgh - Bishopton

Junction	Westbound	Eastbound
8	No access from M73 (southbound) or from A8 (eastbound) & A89	No exit to M73 (northbound) or to A8 (westbound) & A89
9	Access only, no exit	Exit only, no access
13	Access only from M80 (southbound)	Exit only to M80 (northbound)
14	Access only, no exit	Exit only, no access
16	Exit only to A804	Access only from A879
17	Exit only to A82	No restriction
18	Access only from A82 (eastbound)	Exit only to A814
19	No access from A814 (westbound)	Exit only to A814 (westbound)
20	Exit only, no access	Access only, no exit
21	Access only, no exit	Exit only to A8
22	Exit only to M77 (southbound)	Access only from M77 (northbound)
23	Exit only to B768	Access only from B768
25	No access or exit from or to A8	No access or exit from or to A8
25A	Exit only, no access	Access only, no exit
28	Access only, no exit	Exit only, no access
28A	Exit only to A737	Access only from A737

M9 Edinburgh - Dunblane

Junction	Northwestbound	Southeastbound
2	Access only, no exit	Exit only, no access
3	Exit only, no access	Access only, no exit
6	Access only, no exit	Exit only to A905
8	Exit only to M876 (southwestbound)	Access only from M876 (northeastbound)

M73 East of Glasgow

Junction	Northbound	Southbound
2	No access from or exit to A89. No access from M8 (eastbound)	No access from or exit to A89. No exit to M8 (eastbound)

M74 and A74(M) Glasgow - Gretna

Junction	Northbound	Southbound
3	Exit only, no access	Access only, no exit
3A	Access only, no exit	Exit only, no access
7	Access only, no exit	Exit only, no access
9	No access or exit	Exit only, no access
10	No restrictions	Access only, no exit
11	Access only, no exit	Exit only, no access
12	Exit only, no access	Access only, no exit
18	Exit only, no access	Access only, no exit

M77 South of Glasgow

Junction	Northbound	Southbound
with M8 (Jct 22)	No exit to M8 (westbound)	No access from M8 (eastbound)
4	Access only, no exit	Exit only, no access
6	Access only, no exit	Exit only, no access
7	Access only, no exit	No restriction

M80 Glasgow - Stirling

Junction	Northbound	Southbound
4A	Exit only, no access	Access only, no exit
6A	Access only, no exit	Exit only, no access
8	Exit only to M876 (northeastbound)	Access only from M876 (southwestbound)

M90 Forth Road Bridge - Perth

Junction	Northbound	Southbound
2A	Exit only to A92 (eastbound)	Access only from A92 (westbound)
7	Access only, no exit	Exit only, no access
8	Exit only, no access	Access only, no exit
10	No access from A912. No exit to A912 (southbound)	No access from A912 (northbound). No exit to A912

M876 Bonnybridge - Kincardine Bridge

Junction	Northeastbound	Southwestbound
with M80 (Jct 5)	Access only from M80 (northbound)	Exit only to M80 (southbound)
with M9 (Jct 8)	Exit only to M9 (eastbound)	Access only from M9 (westbound)

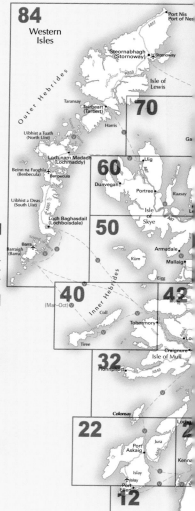

84 Western Isles

70

60

50

40 (Mar–Oct)

42

32

22

12

Port Nis
Port of Ness
Steornabhagh (Stornoway) Stornoway
Isle of Lewis
Taransay
Tairbeart (Tarbert)
Harris
Uibhist a Tuath (North Uist)
Loch-nam Madadh (Lochmaddy)
Uig
Beinn na Faoghla (Benbecula) Benbecula
Dunvegan
Portree
Raasay
Uibhist a Deas (South Uist)
Loch Baghasdail (Lochboisdale)
Isle of Skye
Barra Barraigh (Barra)
Armadale
Rùm
Mallaig
Eigg
Inner Hebrides
Coll
Tobermory
Tiree
Fionnphort
Isle of Mull
Craignure
Colonsay
Loch
Port Askaig
Jura
Kenn
Islay
Islay
Port Ellen
Campbeltown

NORTHERN IRELAND

Larne

BELFAST

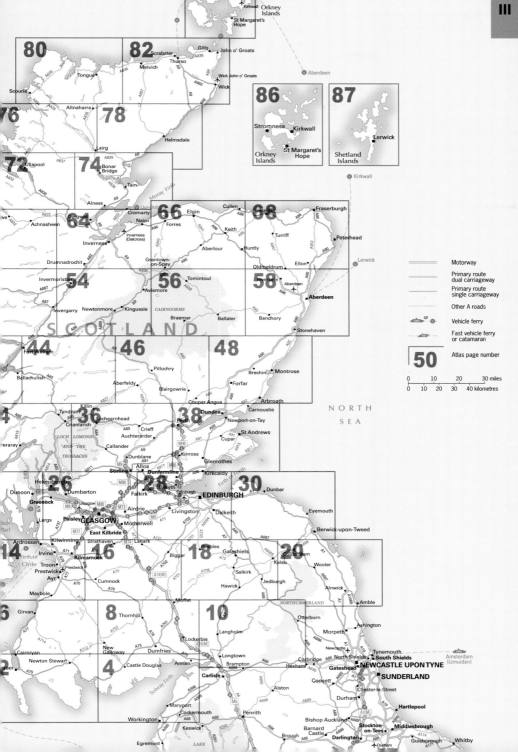

Motorway

Primary route dual carriageway

Primary route single carriageway

Other A roads

Vehicle ferry

Fast vehicle ferry or catamaran

Atlas page number

0   10   20   30 miles

0   10   20   30   40 kilometres

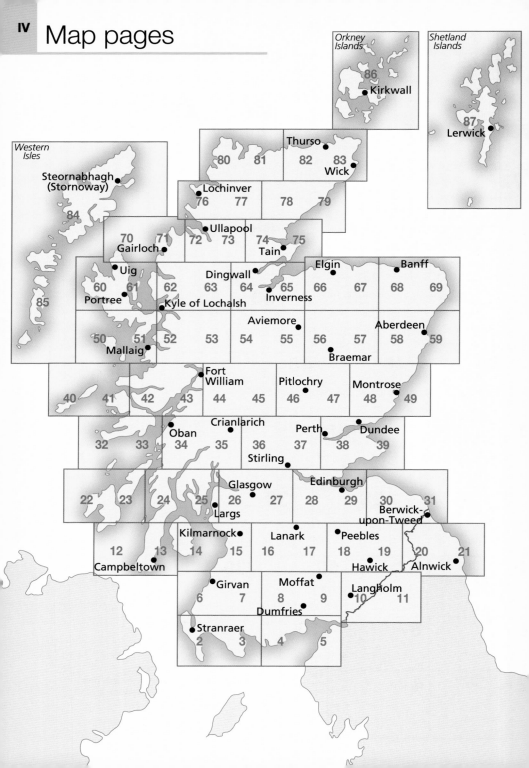

Orkney Islands

86 Kirkwall

Shetland Islands

87 Lerwick

Western Isles

Steornabhagh (Stornoway)

84

85

Thurso
80 81 82 83 Wick

Lochinver
76 77 78 79

70 71 72 Ullapool 73 74 75
Gairloch Tain

60 61 Uig Dingwall Elgin Banff
Portree 62 63 64 65 66 67 68 69
Kyle of Lochalsh Inverness

Aviemore Aberdeen
50 51 52 53 54 55 56 57 58 59
Mallaig Braemar

40 41 42 43 Fort 44 45 Pitlochry 46 47 48 Montrose 49
William

Crianlarich Perth Dundee
32 33 Oban 34 35 36 37 38 39
Stirling

22 23 24 25 26 Glasgow 27 28 Edinburgh 29 30 31
Largs Berwick-upon-Tweed

Kilmarnock Lanark Peebles
12 13 14 15 16 17 18 19 20 21
Campbeltown Hawick Alnwick

Girvan Moffat Langholm
6 7 8 9 10 11
Stranraer Dumfries
2 3 4 5

Atlas symbols

M8	Motorway with number
	Motorway junction with and without number
	Restricted motorway junctions
S Stirling	Motorway service area
	Motorway and junction under construction
A93	Primary route single/dual carriageway
	Primary route junction with and without number
	Restricted primary route junctions
S	Primary route service area
DUNDEE	Primary route destination
A980	Other A road single/dual carriageway
B979	B road single/dual carriageway

	Minor road, more than 4 metres wide, less than 4 metres wide
	Roundabout
	Interchange/junction
	Narrow primary/other A/B road with passing places
	Road under construction
	Road tunnel
Toll	Road toll, steep gradient (arrows point downhill)
5	Distance in miles between symbols
	Railway line, in tunnel
	Railway station and level crossing
	Tourist railway
628 637 Lecht Summit	Height in metres, mountain pass

	City, town, village or other built-up area
30	Safety camera site (fixed location) with speed limit in mph
40	Section of road with two or more fixed safety cameras, with speed limit in mph
50 50	Average speed (SPECS™) camera system with speed limit in mph
or V	Vehicle ferry
	Fast vehicle ferry or catamaran
✈ H	Airport, heliport
F	International freight terminal
H	24-hour Accident & Emergency hospital
C	Crematorium
P•R	Park and Ride (at least 6 days per week)
	National boundary, county/administrative boundary

	Scenic route
	Tourist Information Centre (all year/seasonal)
	Visitor or heritage centre
	Abbey, cathedral or priory
	Ruined abbey, cathedral or priory
✗	Castle
	Historic house or building
	Museum or art gallery
	Industrial interest
	Aqueduct or viaduct
	Garden, arboretum
	Country park

	Agricultural showground
	Theme park
	Farm or animal centre
	Zoological or wildlife collection
	Bird collection, aquarium
	RSPB site
	National Nature Reserve
	Local nature reserve
	Scottish Wildlife Trust reserve
	Forest drive
	National trail
	Viewpoint, picnic site

	Hill-fort
	Prehistoric monument
	Roman antiquity
1719	Battle site with year
	Steam railway centre
	Cave
	Windmill, monument
	Golf course (AA listed)
	Rugby Union national stadium
	International athletics stadium
	Horse racing, show jumping
	Air show venue, motor-racing circuit

	Ski slope (natural, artificial)
	Caravan site (AA inspected)
▲	Camping site (AA inspected)
	Caravan & camping site (AA inspected)
	National Trust for Scotland property
	Historic Scotland site
	Major shopping centre, other place of interest
	Attraction within urban area
	World Heritage Site (UNESCO)
	National Park and National Scenic Area
	Forest Park
	Heritage coast

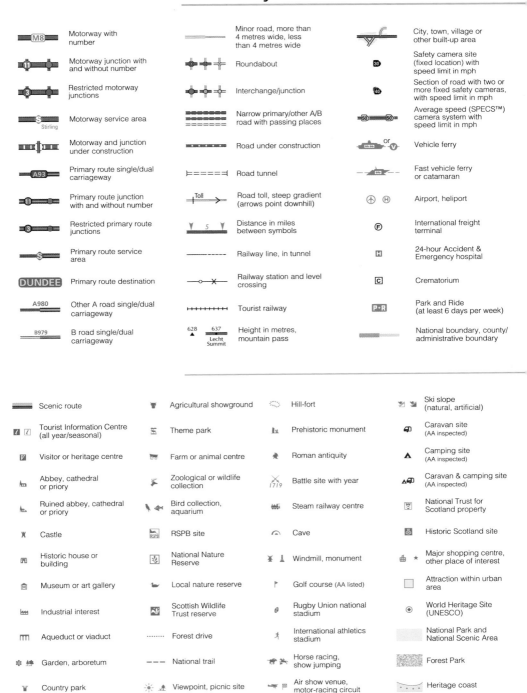

2

Belfast

Larne

Milleur Point

Corsewall Point

Barnhills

Portencalzie

Lady Bay

CARLOCKHILL 321

Glen App

ALTIMEG 387

BENBRAKE HILL 305

Southern Upland Way

Laggangairn Standing Stones

Kirkcolm

Loch Connell

Ervie

Low Barbeth

Cairnryan

Penwhirn Reservoir

Glenwhilly

ARTFIELD FELL 271

Knocknain

Low Salchrie

Leswalt

B7043

Loch Ryan

Braid Fell

New Luce

Castle of St John

Stranraer

A77

A751

Innermessan

Black Loch

White Loch

Castle Kennedy

Chlenry

CRAIG FELL 164

Auchnotteroch

Aird

Castle Kennedy

A75

Portslogan

Broadsea Bay

B738

Glenwhan

Glenluce Abbey

Dunragit

Whitecrook

Glenluce

60

Black Head

Dunskey

Lochans

CAIRN PAT 181

Kildrochet House

Piltanton Burn

B7077

B7084

Ringdoo Point

Milton

Stairhaven

Portpatrick

A77

Stoneykirk

North Milmain

B7084

A716

B7042

Auchenmalg

Mull of Sinniness

Auchenmalg Bay

Sandhead

A716

Cairngarroch

Kirkmadrine Stones

Money Head

High Ardwell

Ardwell Bay

Ardwell House

Ardwell

Chapel Rossan

Drumbreddon

Logan

Balgowan

L U C E   B A Y

Port Logan Bay

Port Logan

Garrochtrie

Clanyard Bay

B7065

A716

Kilstay

Laggantalluch Head

Barncorkrie

Kirkmaiden

Drummore

Killiness Point

Damnaglaur

High Drummore

B7041

Maryport

Cardryne

Cardrain

West Cairngaan

MULL OF GALLOWAY

0   1   2   3   4 miles

0 1 2 3 4 5 kilometres

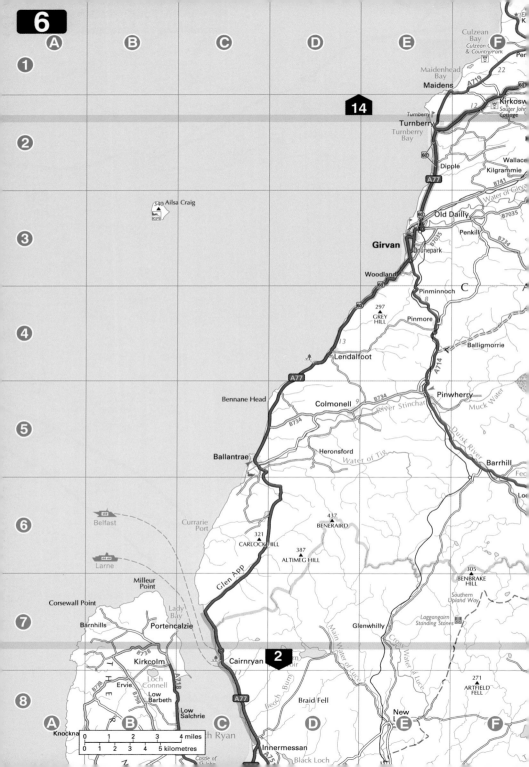

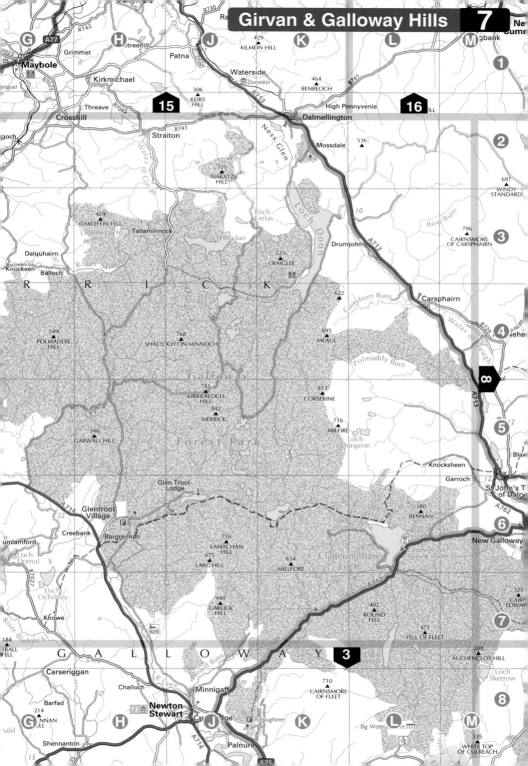

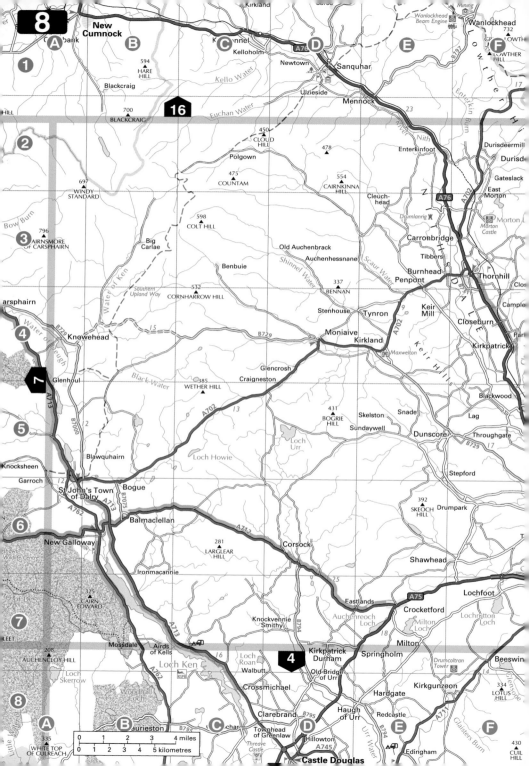

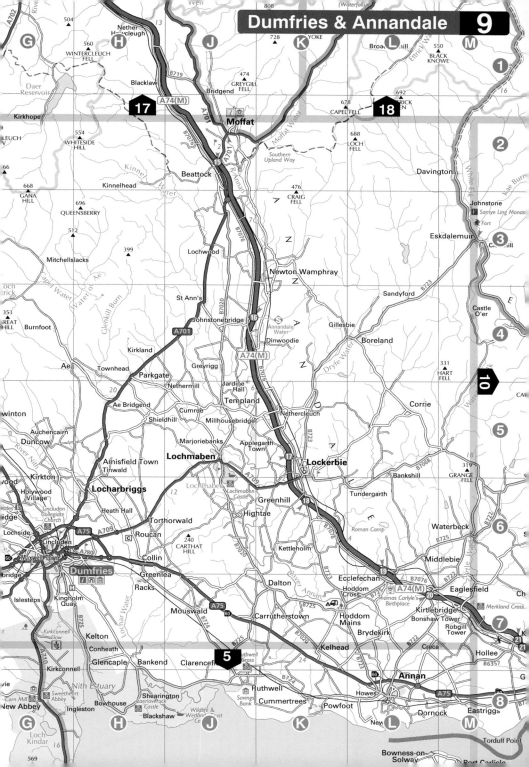

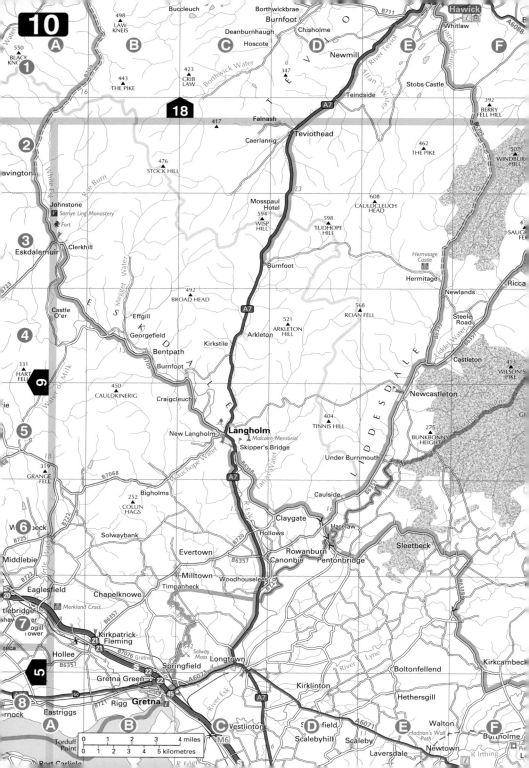

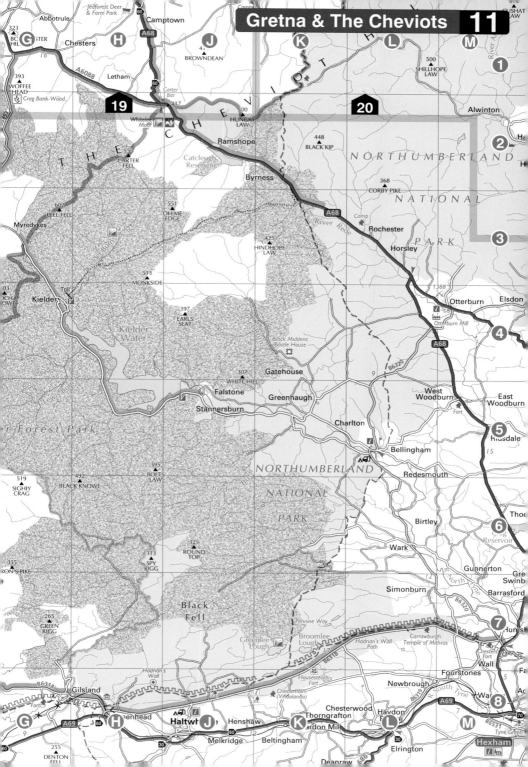

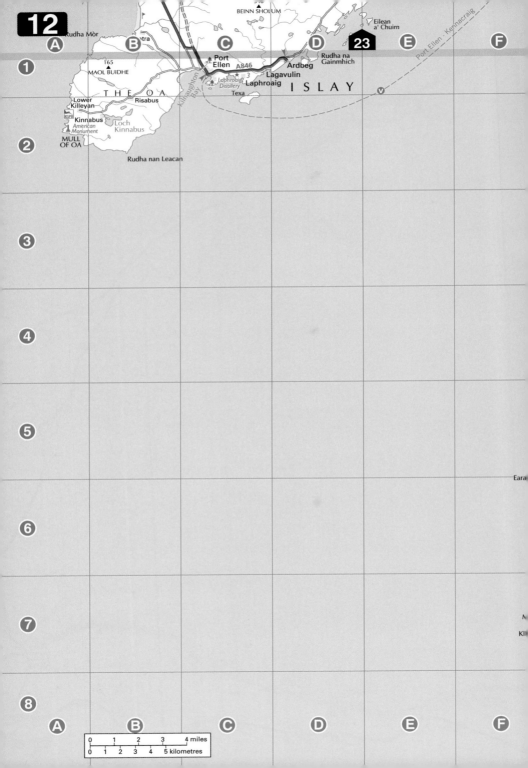

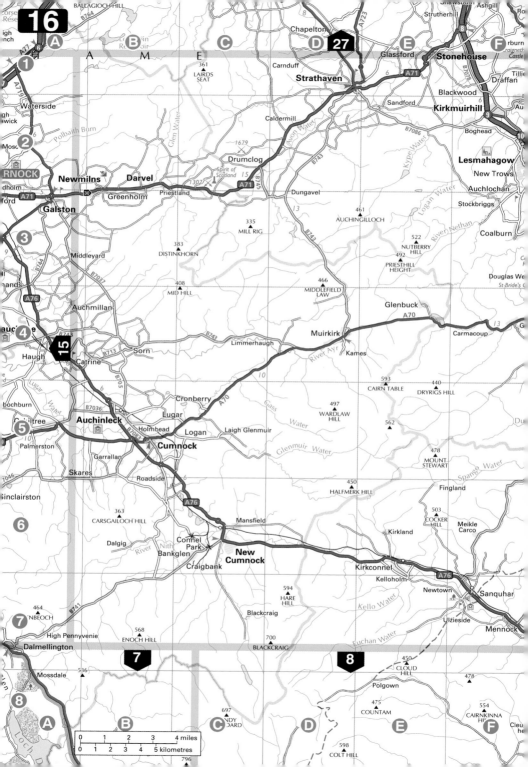

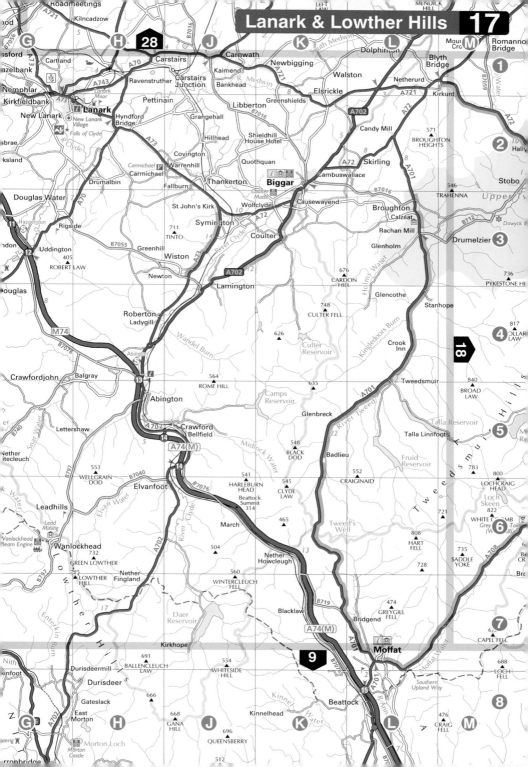

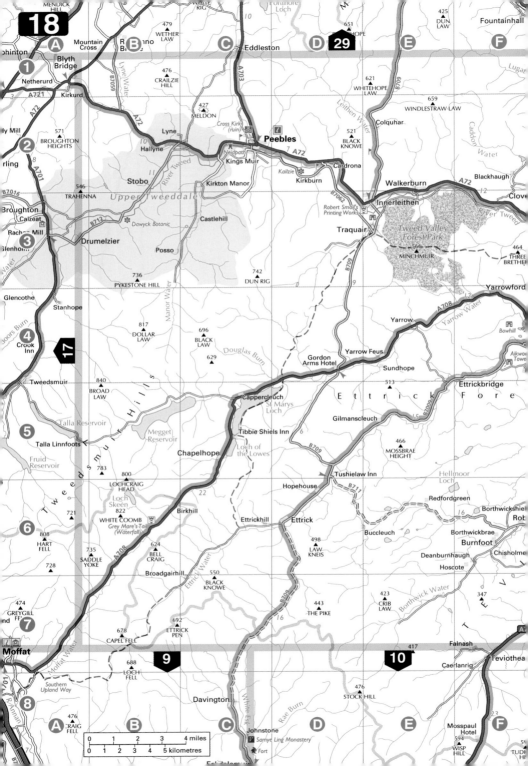

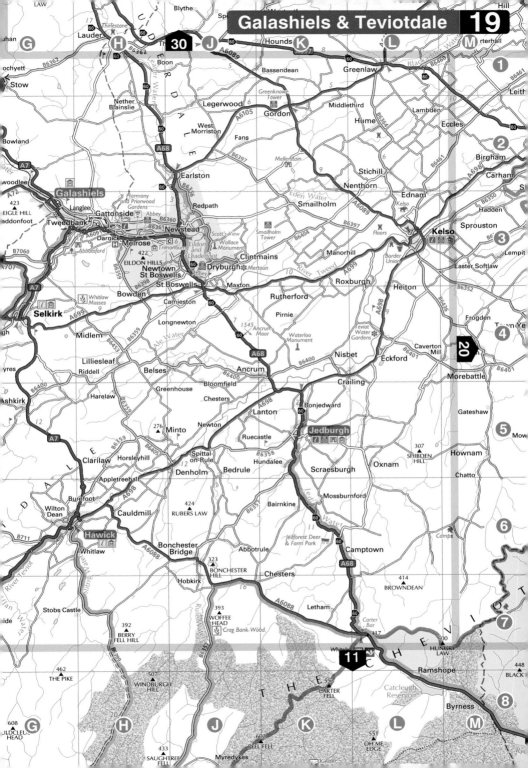

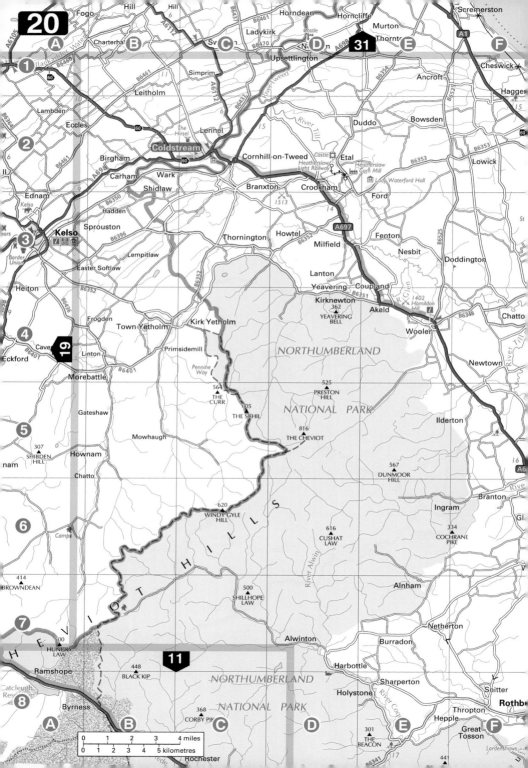

G **H** **J** **K** **L** **M**

1
2
3
4
5
6
7
8

CAUSEWAY
FLOODED
AT HIGH TIDE

HOLY ISLAND

Holy
Island
Lindisfarne
Priory
Lindisfarne
Castle
Castle Point
Guile Point

Longstone
Lighthouse

FARNE
ISLANDS

Staple
Sound

Inner
Sound

North Northumberland
Heritage Coast

Belford

Budle
Bay

Bamburgh
B1342
Bamburgh
B1340

B6349

B6348

Seahouses

North Sunderland

Lucker

Beadnell

Warenford

Swinhoe

Beadnell
Bay

A1

Newstead
Chathill
Tughall
Ellingham
Preston
Preston
Pele Tower

Cattle
Park

Ros
Castle

267
CATERAN
HILL

d Bewick

B6346

North
Charlton

Fallodon

Christon
Bank

Newton-by-the-Sea
Embleton &
Newton Links

Embleton

Embleton
Bay
Dunstanburgh Castle

South
Charlton

Eglingham

Rock
Rennington
Stamford

Dunstan

Craster

Beanley

Howick
Hall

Howick

Cullernose Point

River Aln

Denwick

Longhoughton

Boulmer

Bolton

Alnwick

B6341

Lesbury

Seaton Point

Castle

Edlingham

Alnmouth

Alnmouth
Bay

A1

A1068

Shilbottle

260
GLANTLEES
HILL

Newton-on-
the-Moor

Warkworth Castle
& Hermitage

Warkworth

Amble

Coquet Island

Swarland

Guyzance

Gloster Hill

High
Hauxley

G ramlington
H Felton
J
Acklington
Togston
K Broomhill
L
M

Pauperhaugh

B6344

East
Thirston

South
Broomhill
Red Row

Drindge Bay

West
Thirston

Brinkburn

B6341

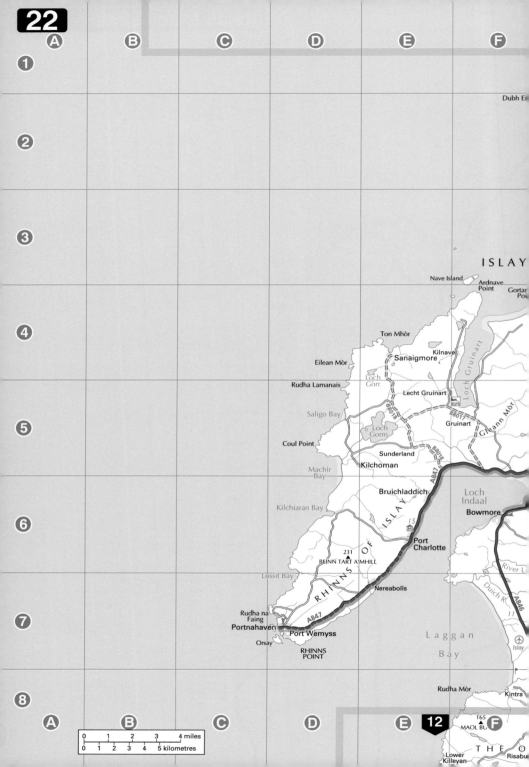

ISLAY

Dubh Ei

Nave Island
Ardnave
Point
Gortar
Poi

Ton Mhòr
Kilnave
Sanaigmore

Eilean Mòr
Loch
Gòrr
Lecht Gruinart

Rudha Lamanais
B8017
Loch Gruinart
Gleann Mòr

Saligo Bay
Loch
Gorm
B8017
Gruinart

Coul Point
Sunderland
B8018

Machir
Bay
Kilchoman
A847

Bruichladdich
Loch
Indaal

Kilchiaran Bay
RHINNS
15
Bowmore

231
BEINN TART A'MHILL
OF
Port
Charlotte

Lossit Bay
ISLAY
River L

Nereabolls
Duich R
A846

Rudha na
Faing
A847
11

Portnahaven
Laggan
Islay

Orsay
Port Wemyss
Bay

RHINNS
POINT

Rudha Mòr
Kintra

165
MAOL BU
THE O
Lower
Killeyan
Risabu

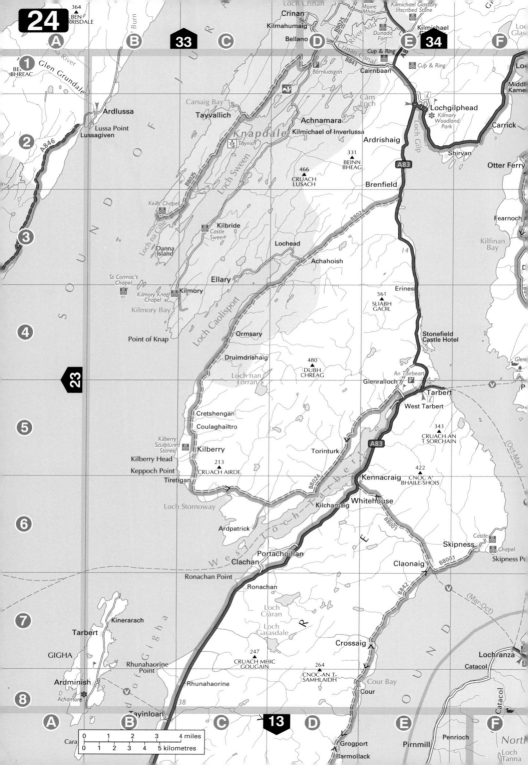

Bac Mòr or Dutchmans Cap

A **B** **C** eag **D** **41** **E** **F**

Staffa
Little Colonsay
Inch Kenneth
Inchkenneth Chapel
(ruin)

1

Fingal's Cave

*Loch na Keal,
Isle of Mull*

2

491
CREACH BHEINN

Fossil Tree

Burg

Rudha nan Cearc

LOC

IONA
Iona Abbey
& Nunnery

Kintra

Loch na
Lathaich

3

Baile Mòr
MacLean's Cross

Fionnphort
(Mar–Oct)

Aridhglas

A849

St Columba
Exhibition
Centre

Bunessan

Loch Assapol

CRU
M

ROSS OF MULL

Soa Island

Erraid

Ardchiavaig

Uisken

Rudh
Braith

4

Rudha
Ardalanish

Torran Rocks

5

6

Eilean
Dubh

Kiloran Bay

Balnahard Rudh'

COLONSAY

7

Kiloran

Kilchattan

Scalasaig

B8086

B8086

Machrins

B8085

Colonsay

8

A **B** **C** **D** **23** **E** Gar **F**

Oronsay

Rudha
Bàn

Dubh Eilean

Eilean

0 1 2 3 4 miles
0 1 2 3 4 5 kilometres

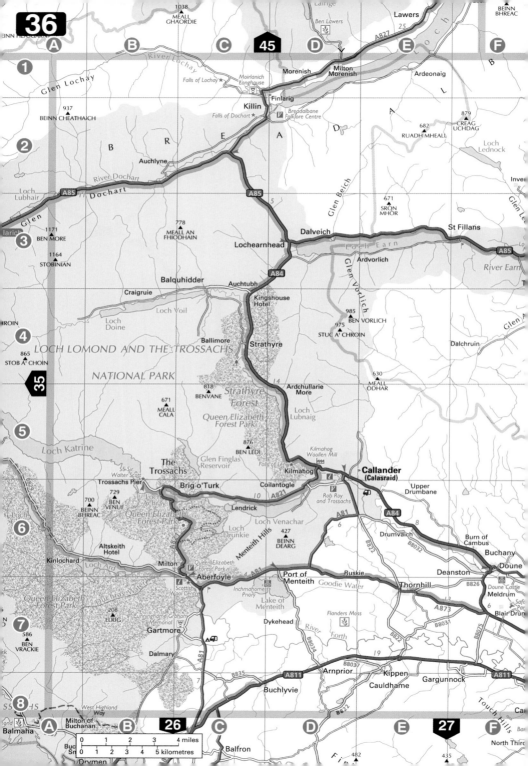

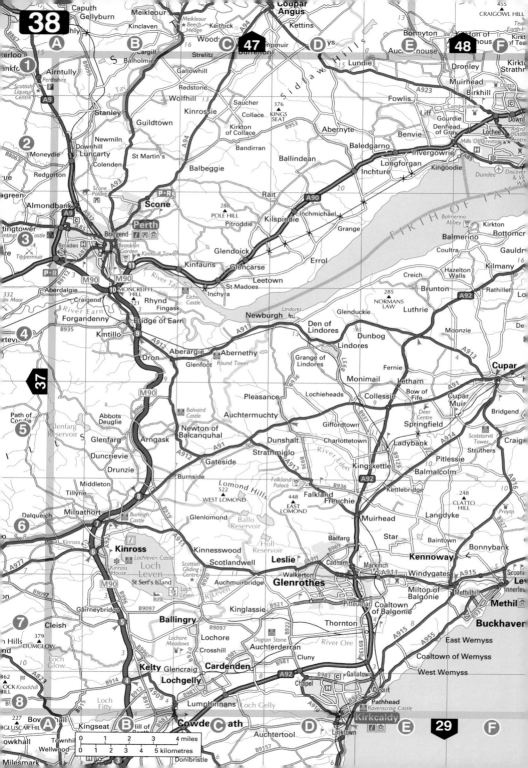

A B C D E F

1

2

3

4

Arna
Grishipoll
Clabhach
Hogh Bay   Ballyhaugh
Totronald
5   Bagh a Chaisteil
(Castlebay)   Coll   Acha
Feall   Arileod
Bay   Uig
Calgary Point   Crossapol
Bay   Rudha
Gunna   Fàsachd

6   Caoles   Rudha Dubh
Rudha Port   B8069
Bhiosd   Clachan   Ruaig
Loch   Mor   Balephetrish
Bhasapoll   Bay
Haugh   Gott
Bay   Ballevullin Cornoigmore   Kenovay   Bay
Kilkenneth   Tiree
7   Middleton Moss   Heylipoll   Scarinish
Barrapoll   B8065
Crossapoll   TIREE
Loch a   B8065
Phuill   Balemartine   Hynish Bay
Rinn   B8067   Mannel
Thorbhais
Balephuill Hynish
Bay

8

A B C D E F

G H **50** J K L M

1
2

MUCK
Port Mor

Eilean
nan Each

Sanna Point

Sanna Bay
Portuairk   Achnaha
Ardnamurchan
Point
Achosnich

Kilmory   Ockle
Branault **3**
436
MEALL NAN CON   ARDNAMU

Ockle
Point

342
BEINN
NA SEILG
Kilchoan
Ormsaigmore   Mingary
Loch
Mudle   **4**
527
BEN
HIANT

Ardslignish

Bagh a Chaisteil
(Castlebay)
Loch Baghasdail
(Lochboisdale)

Eilean Mòr
Rudha
Mòr
Rudha
Sgor-innis
Bousd   Sorisdale

Ardmore Point   Auliston
Point   Or
42

Coll - Oban

COLL

Sorne
Point
Quinish Point

Glengorm Castle   Tobermory
Calve
Island   **5**
Drin

Eilean
Ornsay

Caliach Point

292
'S AIRDE
BEINN

Dervaig
Achnadrish House

A848

Calgary
5
B8073

Calgary Bay

Treshnish Point   Ensay
342
CARN MÒR

ISLE
OF
MULL

444
SPEINNE MÒR   **6**

10

Rudh' a' Chaoil

Burg   Fanmore
390
CNOC AN DÀ CHINN

Glen Aros
Glenaros House   Ard

Fladda

Lunga

Gometra

Ballygown
Eas Fors (Waterfall)

ULVA   Oskamull
19
B8073   333
BEINN
NAN CÀRN   Killiechronan   **7**
B8035
2
Gruline
Macquarie
Mausoleum

TRESHNISH
ISLES

Bac Mòr or Dutchmans Cap
Bac Beag

Little Colonsay

Loch na Keal,
Isle of Mull

Eorsa

591
BEINN A' GH...   **8**

G H **32** J K L M
Staffa
Fingal's Cave

Inchkenneth
Inchkenneth ...pel ...
(ruin)

Balnahard

17

966   70

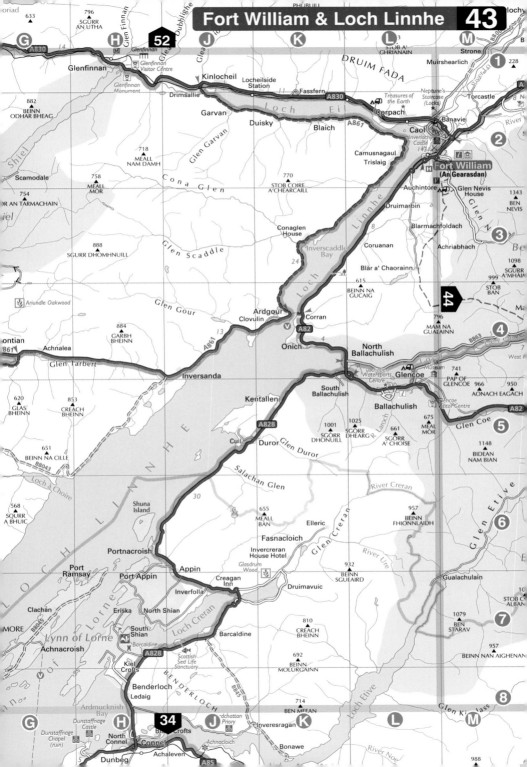

G 54 **H** **J** **K** **L** 94 **M**

A86

747
BINNEIN
SHUAS

1049
GEAL
CHÀRN

896
MEALL
CRUAIDH

769
CREAGAN
MÒR

CÀRN NA CAIM

Loch an Dùin ①

Loch
Pattack

1088
BEINN
A' CHLACHAIR

1034
CÀRN
DEARG

975
A' MHARCONAICH

459
Drumochter
Summit

926
GLAS
MHEALL MÒR ②

Loch Ericht

1101
BEINN
EIBHINN

1008
BEINN UDLAMAIN

991
SGAIRNEACH
MHOR

Dalnaspidal

20

Dalnacardoch

1145
BEN
ALDER

Loch Garry

Glen Garry ③

844
MEALL A'BHEALAICH

Loch
Con

952
SGOR
GAIBHRE

Loch
Errochty

Trinafour
511

R Ericht

864
BEINN PHARIAGAIN

626
SRON A
CHLAONAIDH

841
BEINN
MHOLACH

892
BEINN
A' CHUALLAICH

Glen E...

TORR
DUBH ④

Tay Fo...

46

B847

7 B846

R Tummel

Tummel
Bridge

annoch
tation

Dunan
B846

Bridge
of Ericht

Killichonan

Loch Rannoch

Kinloch
Rannoch

Drumchastle

Dunalastair

Dunalastair
Water

Finnart

Inverhadden

Tempar

Loch
Eigheach

Bridge
of Gaur

Carie

Camghouran

Tay Forest Park

1081
SCHIEHALLION ⑤

Loch Rannoch and Glen Lyon

Glengoulandie
Deer Park

745
MEALL A' MHUIC

1027
CÀRN
GORM

1042
CÀRN
MAIRG

931
MEALL
BUIDHE

860
CAM CHREAG

824
BEINN
DEARG

Ke... ⑥
urn

Loch an
Daimh

Glen Lyon

River Lyon

Bridge of Balgie

Fortingall

Tay
Forest
Park

908
BEINN NAN OIGHREAG

780
MEALL
LUAIDHE

924
MEALL A' CHOIRE
LEITH

1116
MEALL
GARBH

1000
MEALL
GREIGH

Fearnan

Kenmore

Acharn

1038
MEALL
GHAORDIE

Lochan na
Làirige

1214
BEN LAWERS

...annoch
...tre ⑦

Leckbuie
713
BEINN
BHREAC

Ben Lawers

Lawers

Loch Tay

A827
25

SRON A' CH... ⑧

937

River Lochay

Glen Lochay

Falls of Lochay ★

Mon...
Longhouse

J 36

...renish

Milton
Morenish

K

Ardeo...

L

86...

M

Finlarig

Killin

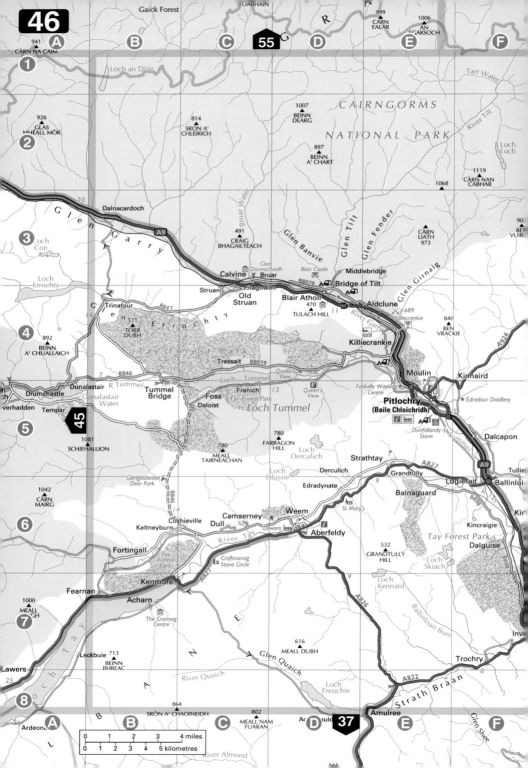

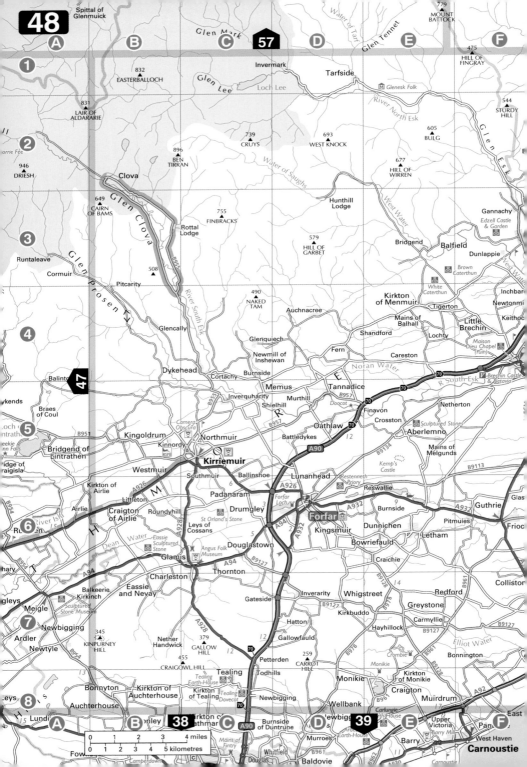

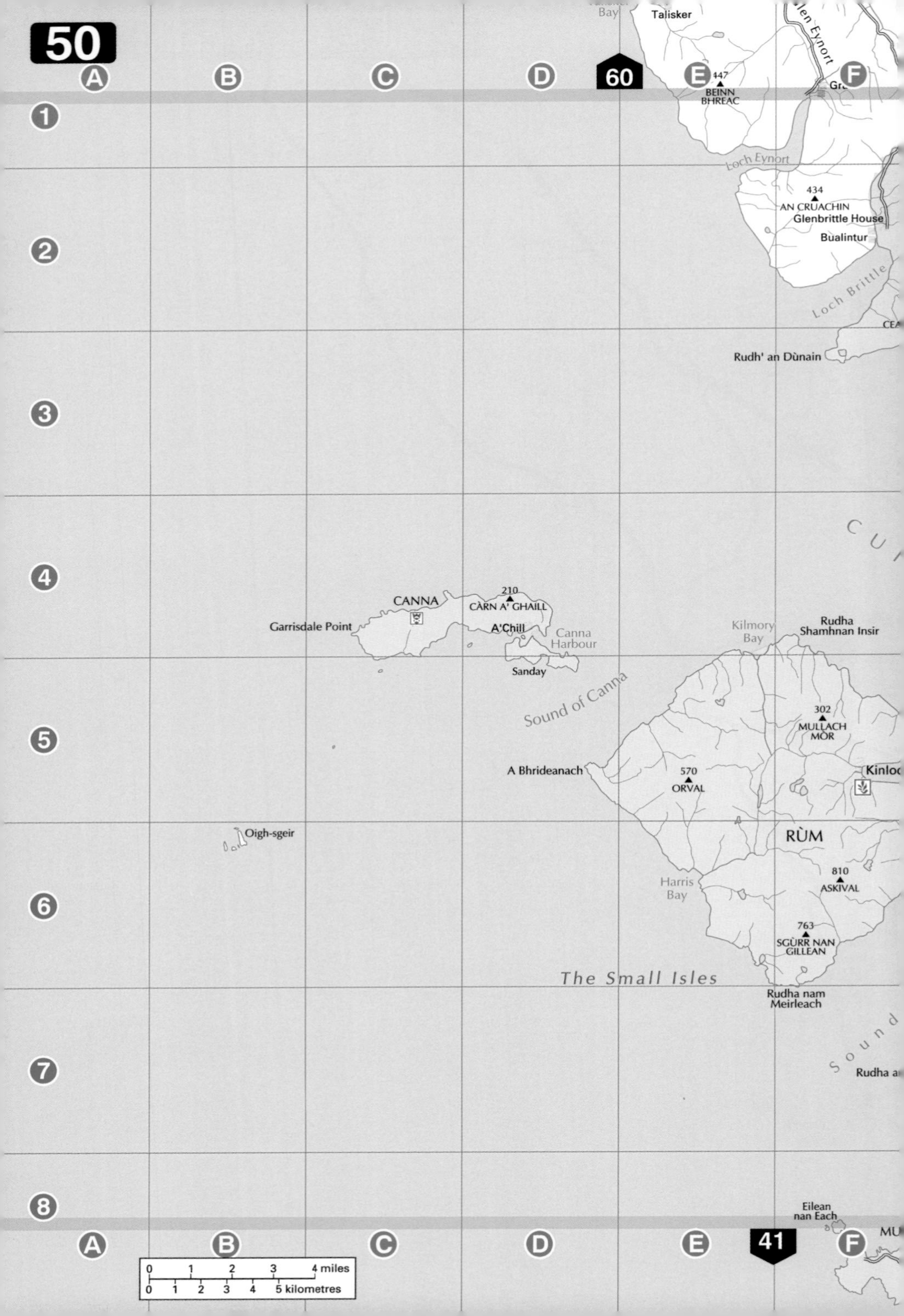

Bay Talisker

Ⓐ
Ⓑ

Loch Eynort

434
AN CRUACHIN
Glenbrittle House
Bualintur

Ⓒ

Loch Brittle

Ⓓ
CEA

Rudh' an Dùnain

Ⓔ

CU

Ⓕ
210
CARN A' GHAILL
CANNA
A'Chill
Garrisdale Point
Canna
Harbour

Kilmory
Bay
Rudha
Shamhnan Insir

Sanday

Sound of Canna

302
MULLACH
MÓR

Ⓖ

A Bhrideanach
570
ORVAL

Kinloc

Oigh-sgeir

RÙM

810
ASKIVAL

Harris
Bay

Ⓗ

763
SGURR NAN
GILLEAN

The Small Isles

Rudha nam
Meirleach

Soun

Ⓘ
Rudha a

Ⓙ

Eilean
nan Each

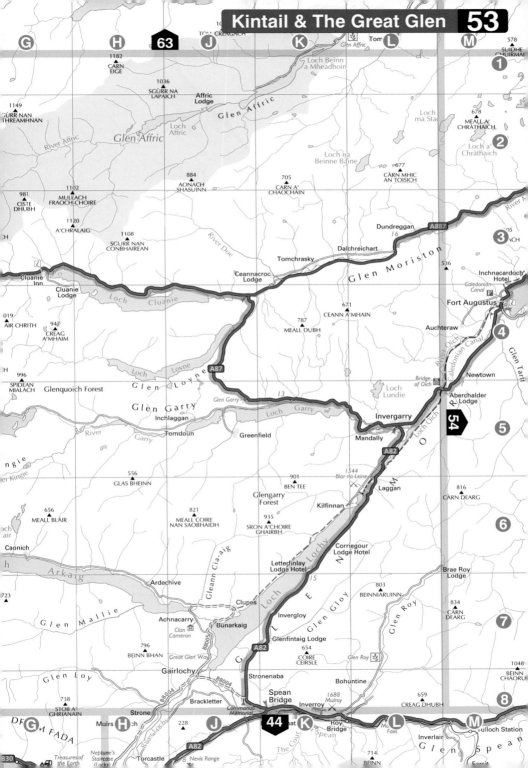

G   **H**   **63**   **J**   **K**   **L**   **M**

TOLL CREAGACH

Glen Affric   Tom

578
SUIDHE
CHUIRMA

1

1182
CARN
EIGE

Loch Beinn
a' Mheadhoin

1036
SGÙRR NA
LAPAICH

Affric
Lodge

Glen Affric

Loch
ma Stac

678
MEALL A'
CHRATHAICH

1149
SGURR NAN
THREAMHNAN

River Affric

Glen Affric

Loch
Affric

Loch a'
Chràthaich

2

884
AONACH
SHASUINN

Loch na
Beinne Bàine

677
CARN MHIC
AN TOISICH

981
CISTE
DHUBH

1102
MULLACH
FRAOCH-CHOIRE

River Doe

705
CARN A'
CHAOCHAIN

705
ACH

3

1120
A'CHRALAIG

1108
SGURR NAN
CONBHAIREAN

Dundreggan
16 **A887**

River Moriston

536

Inchnacardoch
Hotel

Tomchrasky

Dalchreichart

Glen Moriston

Cluanie
Inn

Ceannacroc
Lodge

Caledonian Canal

Cluanie
Lodge

Loch Cluanie

Fort Augustus

019
AIR CHRITH

671
CEANN A'MHAIN

Auchteraw

4

947
CREAG
A'MHAIM

787
MEALL DUBH

River Oich

Glen Tarff

996
SPIDEAN
MIALACH

Glen Loyne

A87

Caledonian Canal

Newtown

Glenquoich Forest

Glen Garry

Glen Garry

13

Bridge
of Oich

Loch
Lundie

Aberchalder
Lodge

5

Inchlaggan

Loch Garry

Invergarry

River Garry

Tomdoun

Greenfield

Mandally

A82

Loch Oich

816
CARN DEARG

ngie
er Kingie

556
GLAS BHEINN

901
BEN TEE

1544
Blar-na-Leine

Laggan

6

656
MEALL BLAIR

Glengarry
Forest

821
MEALL COIRE
NAN SAOBHAIDH

935
SRON A'CHOIRE
GHAIRBH

Kilfinnan

803
BEINNIARUINN

Brae Roy
Lodge

Caonich

Corriegour
Lodge Hotel

834
CARN
DEARG

7

723

Arkaig

Gleann Cia-aig

Letterfinlay
Lodge Hotel

15

Glen Roy

Glen Mallie

Clunes

Invergloy

Glen Gloy

1048
BEINN
CHAORU

Ardechive

796
BEINN BHAN

Achnacarry

Bunarkaig

Clan
Cameron

Glenfintaig Lodge

654
COIRE
CEIRSLE

Glen Roy

659
CREAG DHUBH

8

Glen Loy

738
STOB A'
GHRIANAIN

Great Glen Way

A82

Stronenaba

Bohuntine

Gairlochy

Bohuntine

Spean
Bridge

228

Strone

Bracletter

Commando
Memorial

Inverroy

1688
Mulroy

Inverlair

Glen Spean

830

Muirs

G   DRUIM FADA   **H**   **J**   **44**   **K**   Roy
Bridge   **L**   Falls   **M**   ulloch Station

Neptune's
Staircase
(Locks)

Treasures of
the Earth

Torcastle

A82

Nevis Range

The Cour

Spean

714
BEINN

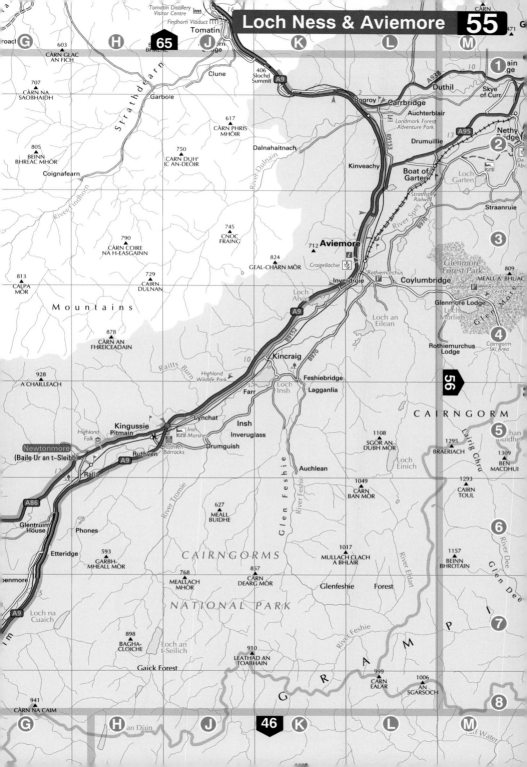

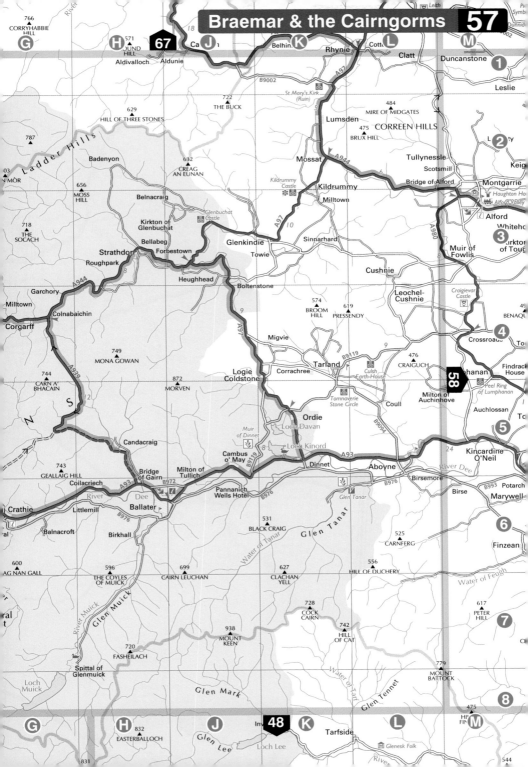

G 67 **H** 571 DUND HILL **J** Ca 18 **K** Belhin **L** Cott **M** **1**
766 CORRYHABBIE HILL

Aldivalloch Aldunie Ca

Rhynie Clatt Duncanstone

Leith

Leslie

B9002 St. Mary's Kirk (Ruin) A97

722 THE BUCK

629 HILL OF THREE STONES

484 MIRE OF MIDGATES

Lumsden 475 BRUX HILL CORREEN HILLS

2

787

Ladder Hills

03 'MÓR

Badenyon

632 CREAG AN EUNAN

Kildrummy Castle

Mossat A944

Tullynessle Scotsmill

Keig

Montgarrie

656 MOSS HILL

Belnacraig

Kildrummy

Milltown

Bridge of Alford

Haughton Ho

Alford Valley

Glenbuchat Castle

Kirkton of Glenbuchat

Bellabeg Forbestown

Glenkindie A97

Towie

Sinnarhard

Cushnie

Alford

3 Whiteho

Kirton of Toug

Muir of Fowlis

718 THE SOCACH

Strathdon Roughpark

Heughhead

Boltenstone

574 BROOM HILL

619 PRESSENDY

Leochel-Cushnie

Craigievar Castle

49

BENAQU

Garchory A944

Colnabaichin

749 MONA GOWAN

9 A97

Migvie

B9119

Tarland Culsh Earth-House

476 CRAIGUCH

Crossroads **4**

To

Corgarff

744 CAIRN 'A' BHACAIN

A939

872 MORVEN

Logie Coldstone

Corrachree

Tomnaverie Stone Circle

Coull

Milton of Auchinhove

Findrack House

58

Auchlossan

To

N S 12

743 GEALLAIG HILL

Candacraig

Muir of Dinnet

Loch Davan

Ordie Loch Kinord

A93

Kincardine O'Neil

5

Coilacriech

Bridge of Gairn

B972

Milton of Tullich

Cambus o' May B9119

Dinnet

Aboyne

Birsemore River Dee

Birse

24

B993 Potarch

Marywell

Crathie Littlemill

River Dee

Ballater

Pannanich Wells Hotel

B976

Glen Tanar

B976

6

Balnacroft Birkhall

531 BLACK CRAIG

Glen Tanar

525 CARNFERG

Finzean

600 AG NAN GALL

596 THE COYLES OF MUICK

699 CAIRN LEUCHAN

627 CLACHAN YELL

556 HILL OF DUCHERY

Water of Feugh

617 PETER HILL

ral

728 COCK CAIRN

742 HILL OF CAT

7

Cl

Glen Muick

River Muick

938 MOUNT KEEN

720 FASHEILACH

Spittal of Glenmuick

779 MOUNT BATTOCK

8

475

Loch Muick

Glen Mark

Glen Tennet

Water of Tarf

G **H** 832 EASTERBALLOCH **J** Glen Lee **48** Inv **K** Tarfside **L** **M** 475 HI FIN

831

Loch Lee

Glenesk Folk

544

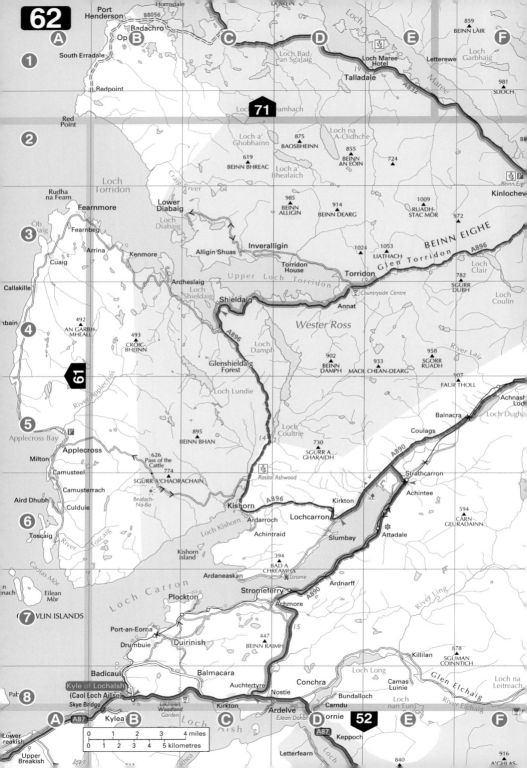

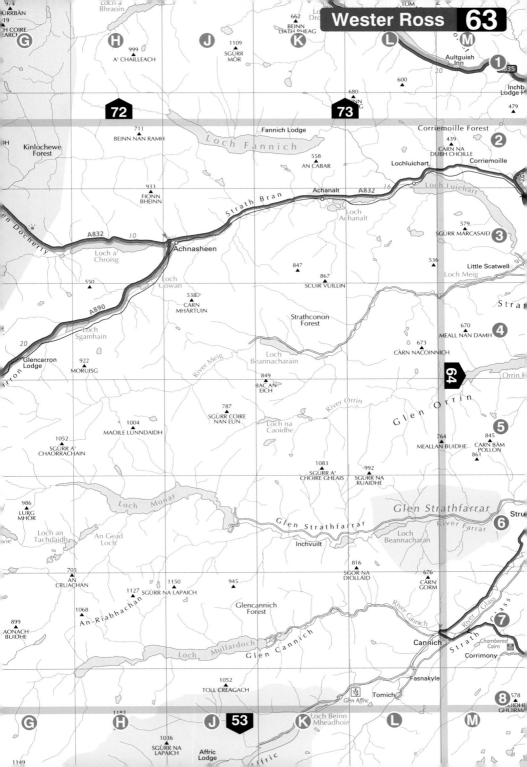

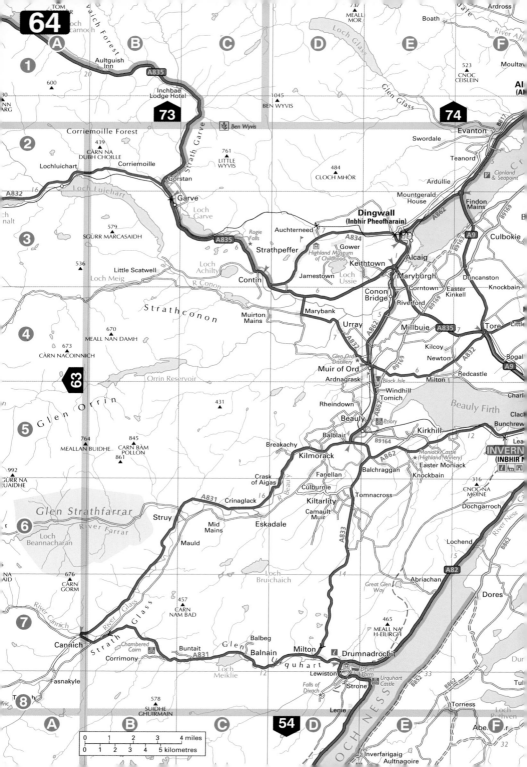

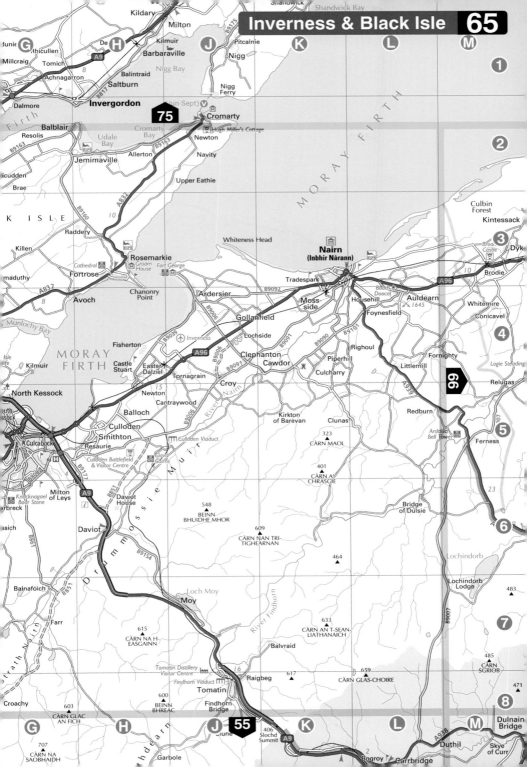

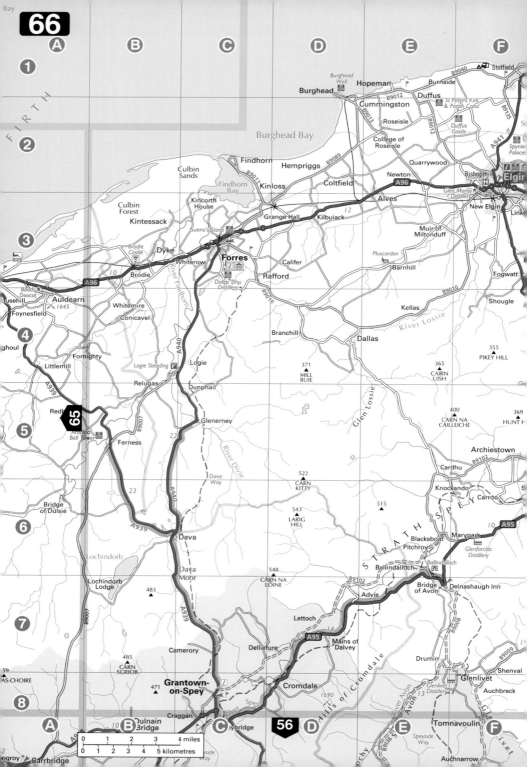

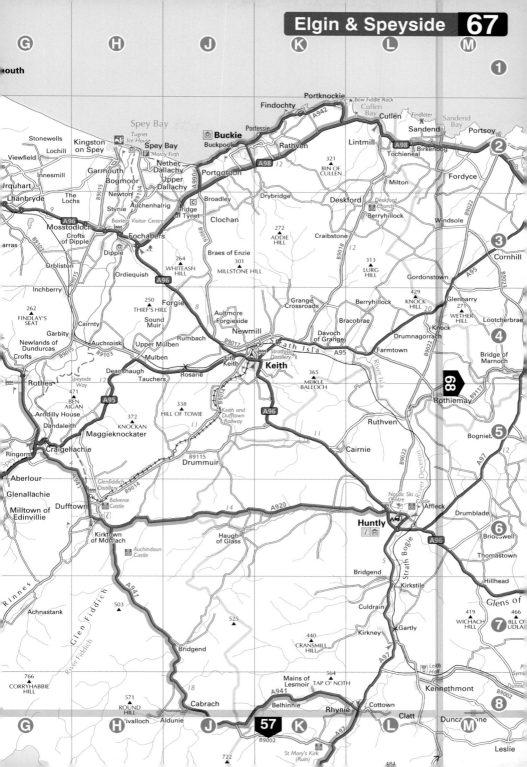

G H J K L M

1

outh

2

Stonewells
Viewfield
Innesmill
rquhart
Lhanbryde
arras

Kingston
on Spey
Lochill
Garmouth
Bogmoor
The Lochs
Newton
Stynie
Auchenhalrig

Spey Bay
Tugnet
Ice House
Spey Bay
Moray Firth
Nether
Dallachy
Upper
Dallachy
Bridge
of Tynet

Buckie
Buckpool
Portgordon
Broadley
Clochan

Portessie
Rathven

Findochty
Portknockie
Bow Fiddle Rock
Cullen
Bay
Cullen
Findlater
Sandend
Sandend
Bay
Portsoy

Lintmill
Tochieneal
Birkenbog
Fordyce

321
BIN OF
CULLEN
Milton

Drybridge
Deskford
Deskford
Church
Berryhillock
Windsole

Mosstodloch
Crofts
of Dipple
Orbliston
Inchberry
Dipple
Ordiequish
Fochabers

272
ADDIE
HILL
Braes of Enzie
264
WHITEASH
HILL
301
MILLSTONE HILL

Craibstone
Gordonstown

313
LURG
HILL
Cornhill

262
FINDLAY'S
SEAT
Garbity
Newlands of
Dundurcas
Crofts
Rothes

250
THIEF'S HILL
Cairnty
Forgie
Sound
Muir
Auchroisk
Upper Mulben
Mulben

Aultmore
Forgieside
Newmill
Rumbach
Fife
Keith
Strathisla
Distillery
Keith

Grange
Crossroads
Berryhillock
Bracobrae
Davoch
of Grange
429
KNOCK
HILL
20
Glenbarry
271
WETHER
HILL
Knock
Drumnagorrach
Farmtown

Lootcherbrae

Bridge of
Marnoch

471
BEN
AIGAN
Arndilly House
Dandaleith
Deanshaugh
Tauchers
Rosarie
338
HILL OF TOWIE
372
KNOCKAN
Maggieknockater

365
MEIKLE
BALLOCH
Ruthven
Cairnie

68
Rothiemay

Bogniet

Craigellachie
Aberlour
Glenallachie
Milltown of
Edinvillie
Ringorm
Dufftown
Glenfiddich
Distillery
Balvenie
Castle
Drummuir
Keith and
Dufftown
Railway

Nordic Ski
Centre
Castle
Affleck
Huntly

Drumblade
Bridgeswell
Thomastown

Achnastank

Kirktown
of Mortlach
Auchindoun
Castle
Haugh
of Glass
Bridgend
Kirkstile
Hillhead
Glens of

503

525
Bridgend
Culdrain
Gartly
Kirkney
419
WICHACH
HILL
466
UDLA

440
CRANSMILL
HILL
766
CORRYHABBIE
HILL
571
ROUND
HILL
Hivalloch
Aldunie
Cabrach

Mains of
Lesmoir
564
TAP O' NOTH
Belhinnie
Rhynie
Cottown
Clatt
Leith
Hall
Kennethmont

722

St Mary's Kirk
(Ruin)
484

8

7

6

5

4

3

G H J K L M

1
2
3
4
5
6
7
8

Rosehearty
Pittulie
Sandhaven
Castle Lighthouse & Museum
Kinnaird Head
Craigiefold
Peathill
Kirktown
Fraserburgh
Fraserburgh Bay
Maggie's Hoosie
Aberdour Bay
Coburby
Percyhorner
Pitblae
Cairnbulg
Inverallochy
Whitelinks Bay
New Aberdour
Boyndlie
Mid Ardlaw
Memsie
St Combs
A98
A981
B9032
Memsie Cairn
Rathen
Newburgh
Lonmay
Crofts of Savoch
Rattray Head
234 WAUGHTON HILL
Loch of Strathbeg
B9093
Strichen
Crimond
Blackhill
New Pitsligo
New Leeds
A952
18
Bonnykelly
B9093
Denhead
Leys
Kirktown
St Fergus
Fetterangus
Backfolds
A90
Rora
Deer Abbey
Dunshillock
River Ugie
Maud
B9106
Mintlaw
Longside
Inverugie
A950
Buchanhaven
Peterhead
New Deer
B9029
Old Deer
Inverquhomery
Peterhead
Blackhill of Clackriach
Bulwark
Stuartfield
Peterhead Bay
Drymuir
Millbreck
Nether Kinmundy
Hillhead of Cocklaw
Burnhaven
Nethermuir
Clola
Blackhill
Stirling
Buchan Ness
Knaven
B9030
Kinnadie
Lendrum Terrace
Boddam
Auchnagatt
Kinknockie
Cairnorrie
Brownhill
Ardallie
Longhaven
Inkhorn
Coldwells
Hatton
Bullers of Buchan
North Haven
Arthrath
Muirtack
Auchiries
A948
A952
Slains
Cruden Bay
Ythanbank
Birness
Bogbrae
Chapel Hill
Bay of Cruden
Whinnyfold
The Skares
Altar-Tomb of William Forbes
Auchedly
Artrochie
Kinharrachie
Ythsie
Ellon
P+R
Esslemont
Kirkton of Logie Buchan
Kirktown of Slains
Collieston
Pitmedden Garden
Pitmedden
Logierieve
Forvie
Housiside
B90
Udny
Udny Station
Pettymuk
Cultercullen
Foveran
Newburgh

A · B · C · D · E · F

1
2
3
4
5
6
7
8

Loch Shell

Loch Collum

SOUND OF SHIANT

SHIANT
ISLANDS

Fladda-chùain

Eilean Trodday

Rudha Hunish

North
Duntulm

Duntulm   Kilmaluag

A855

Lùb Score

Skye Museum
of Island Life   Flodigarry

Borneskitaig   Heribusta   Eilean Flodigarry

Kilmuir   Kilvaxter   542   Polltiel

Balgown   MEAL NA   Digg   Staffin
                  SUIREAMACH   Bay   Staffin Island

                  Brogaig

Linicro   Stenscholl   Staffin

Totscore   464   Kilt Rock Waterfall
                 BIODA   Ellishader
Loch nam Madadh BUIDHE   Trotternish
(Lochmaddy)

Tairbeart
(Tarbert)

60   **61**

Idrigill   Maligar

                 Marishader   Valtos

Uig   River Rha   611   Garros   Rudha nam Brathairean
(Uige)   River Conon   BEINN   Culnaknock
Uig Bay   EDRA

Loch Snizort   Earl   Le   Tote
                                                 A855
Loch S...ort   B   C   D   E   F

Loch a' Bhi...

608

Peinlich

0 1 2 3 4 miles
0 1 2 3 4 5 kilometres

G H J K L M

1
Polbai
Badentarb Bay
Tanera Beg
Tanera Mòr
Hor Islan
Steornabhagh (Stornoway)
Glas-leac Beag
Eilean Dubh
Scorai

2

Priest Island

Cailleach Head
Le

3
Greenstone Point
Rudha Beag
Stattic Point
Badluarach
A832
Badc
GRUINARD ISLAND
Gruinard Bay
Mellon Udrigle
Laide
Litt

4
Rudha Reidh
Foura
Cove
Mellon Charles
Ormiscaig
Aultbea
Gruinard
Little Gruinard River
Gruinard River
347
CREAG-MHEAL BEAG
296
AN CUAIDH
Melvaig
ISLE OF EWE
Loch Fada

72

5
Aultgrishin
Loch Ewe
Inverasdale
293
CNOC BREAC
Naast
Inverewe Garden
13
250
MEALL NA MEINE
Fronn
681
BEINN A' CHAISGEIN BEAG
Wester Ross
North Erradale
Poolewe
Londubh
Dubh Loch

6
Big Sand
Strath
A832
Auchtercairn
Heritage
Smithstown
Lonemore
Gairloch
Charlestown
421
MEALL AN DOIREIN
791
BEINN AIRIDH CHARR
859
BEINN LAIR
Longa Island
Loch Gairloch
Eilean Horrisdale

7
Port Henderson
Badachro
B8056
Opinan
South Erradale
Redpoint
Loch-Bad an Sgalaig
Loch Maree Hotel
Talladale
19
Letterewe
Loch Garbhaig
Maree
981
SLIOCH
Red Point
Loch Ghaineamhach

62
Loch Ghobhain
875
BAOSBHEINN
Loch na A'Oidhche
855
BEINN AN EOIN
724

8
Rudha na Fearn
Loch Torridon
Fearnn
Lower Diabaig
619
BEINN BHREAC
Loch a' Bhealaich
B ALLIGIN
914
BEINN DEARG
1009
RUADH-STAC MOR
972
Kinloch
Beinn E

Òb Chuaig
Fearnbeg
Loch Diabaig
EIGHE

G H J K L M

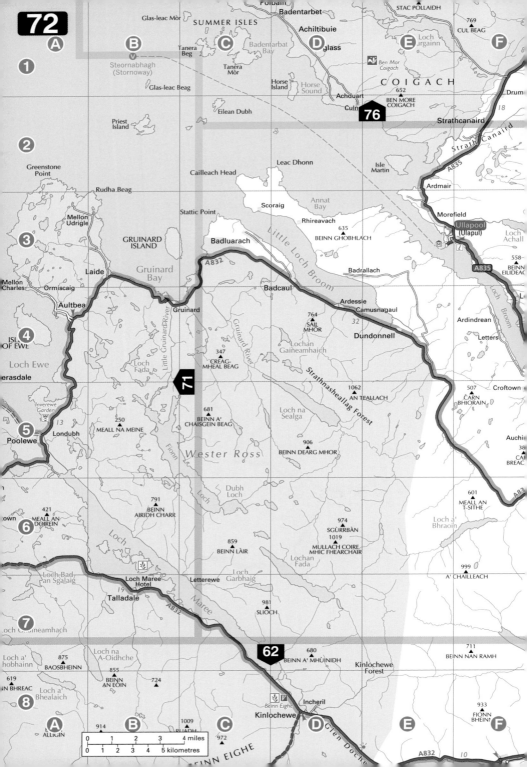

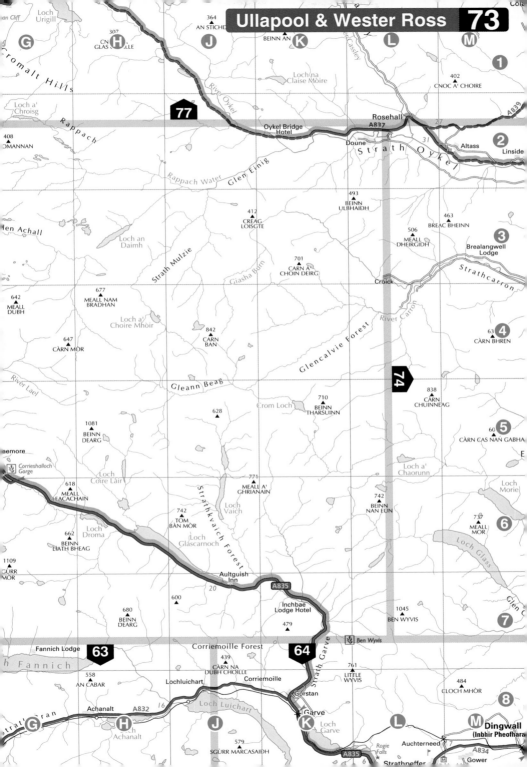

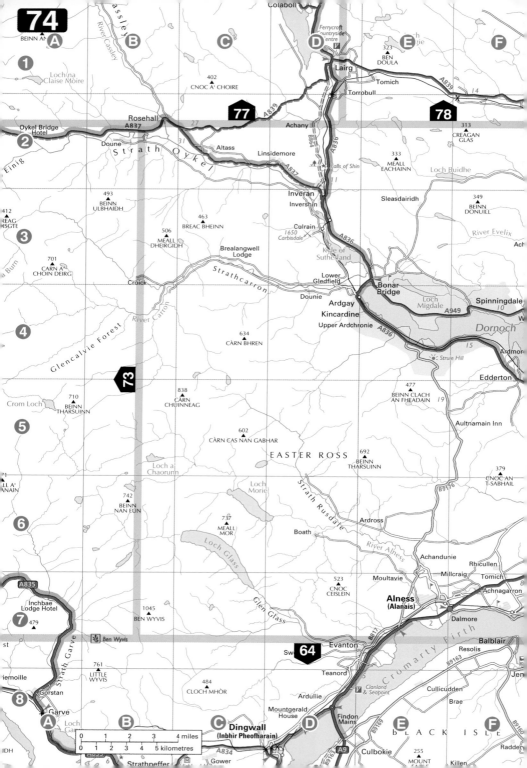

G H J K L M

① ② ③ ④ ⑤ ⑥ ⑦ ⑧

River Brora
Dalreavoch Lodge
Loch Horn
520 ▲ BEN HORN
Dalchalm
Brora

79

Golspie Burn
378 ▲ CAGAR FEOSAIG
Backies
446 ▲ BEN LUNDIE
Carn Liath
Doll
A9

383 ▲ BEN BHRAGGIE
Rhives
Golspie
Dunrobin Castle

orboll

Cambusavie Platform
Loch Fleet
Badninish
Skelbo 7
Skelbo Street
Fourpenny
Embo
Birichin
B9168
Embo Street
Evelix
A949
Pitgrudy
Royal Dornoch
hmore A9 3
Camore
Dornoch
Cuthill
Historylinks

rie
rry Point
Dornoch Firth
Innis Mhor
Tarbat Ness
Brucefield
Wilkhaven

Glenmorangie Distillery
Portmahomack
Morangie
Inver
Rockfield
B9165
284 ▲
Tain
(Baile Dhubhthaich)
Arboll
Toulvaddie
Lochslin
Loch Eye
Rhynie
Hill of Fearn
Newfield
6 B9165
Balmuchy
Hilton of Cadboll
Chapel (ruin)
Fearn
Tullich
Hilton
Arabella
Shandwick
Balintore
Ballchraggan
Ankerville
Shandwick Bay
Kildary
B9175
Milton
Pitcalnie
Kilmuir
Barbaraville
Nigg
alintraid
Nigg Bay
urn
Nigg Ferry

don
(Jun-Sept) V
Cromarty
Hugh Miller's Cottage
Cromarty Bay
Newton
B9163
Allerton
Navity
Upper Eathie

65

66

Burghead
Culbin Sands
Findhorn
Hen
Findhorn Bay
Kincorth House
Culbin Forest
Kintessack
ss
Grange Ha

MORAY FIRTH

G H J K L M

Whiteness Head
Nairn
Brodie Castle
Sueno's Stone
Dyke

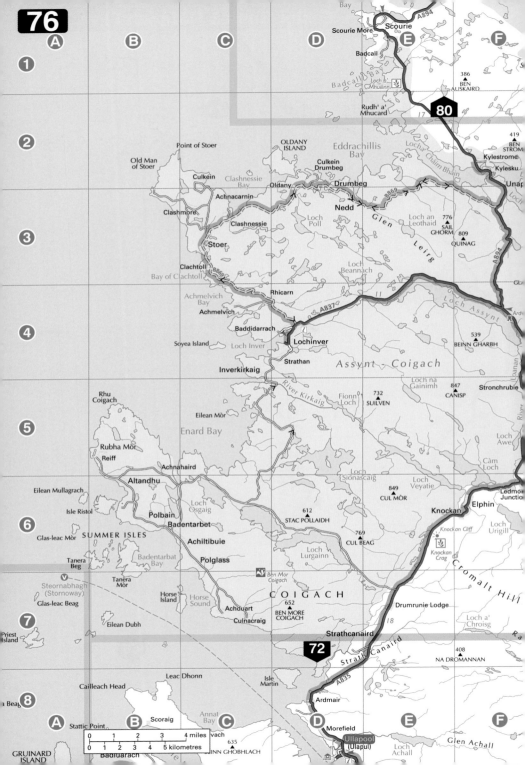

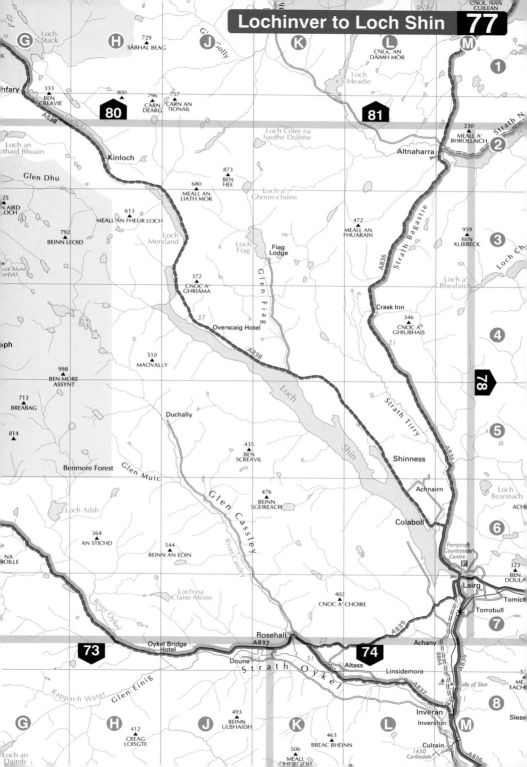

G H J K L M

1

729
SÀBHAL BEAG

G'olly

CNOC NAN
CUILEAN

333
BEN
SCREAVIE

800
CARN
DEARG

796
CARN AN
TIONAIL

757
CARN AN
TIONAIL

80

CNOC AN
DÀIMH MÒR

81

Loch
Meadie

230
MEALL A'
BHROLLAICH

2

Strath N

Altnaharra

Loch Còire na
Saidhe Duibhe

Kinloch

873
BEN
HEE

Loch-a'-
Ghorm-choire

472
MEALL AN
FHUARAIN

959
BEN
KLIBRECK

3

Loch Ch

Glen Dhu

680
MEALL AN
LIATH MOR

Strath Bagastie

Loch an
thaid Bhuain

613
MEALL AN FHEUR LOCH

Loch
Merkland

Loch
Fiag

Fiag
Lodge

Loch a'
Bhealaich

25
N AIRD
OCH

792
BEINN LEOID

372
CNOC A'
GHRIAMA

Crask Inn

346
CNOC A'
GHIUBHAIS

4

ual Aluinn
erfall)

37

Overscaig Hotel

A838

21

510
MAOVALLY

Glen Fiag

78

Loch

ph

998
BEN MORE
ASSYNT

Duchally

Shinness

5

713
BREABAG

Strath Tirry

Shin

814

Benmore Forest

Glen Muic

435
BEN
SCREAVIL

Achnairn

Loch
Beannach

ACH

Loch Ailsh

Glen Cassley

476
BEINN
SGEIREACH

Colaboll

6

NA
OILLE

364
AN STICHD

544
BEINN AN EÒIN

River Cassley

Ferrycroft
Countryside
Centre

323
BEN
DOULA

Loch na
Claise Mòire

402
CNOC A' CHOIRE

Lairg

Tomich

River Oykel

Torrobull

7

73

Oykel Bridge
Hotel

A837

Rosehall

27

A839

74

Achany

Doune

Strath Oykel

31

Altass

B864

Linsidemore

Falls of Shin

A837

ME
EACH

8

Rappach Water

Glen Einig

Inveran

Invershin

Sleas

G

412
CREAG
LOISGTE

H

493
BEINN
ULBHAIDH

J

506
MEALL
DHEIRGIDH

K

463
BREAC BHEINN

L

Culrain

1650
Carbisdale

M

Loch an
Daimh

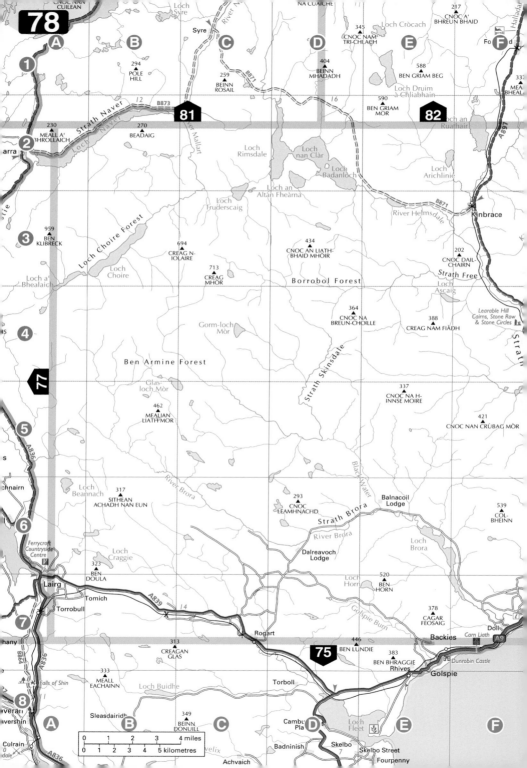

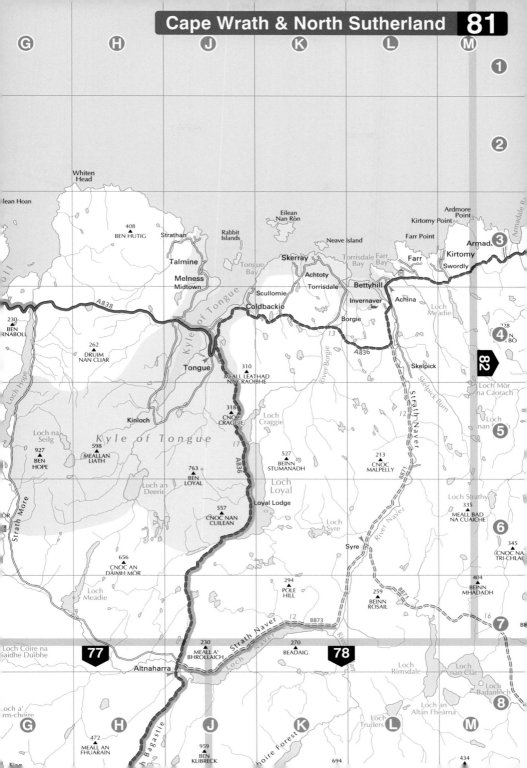

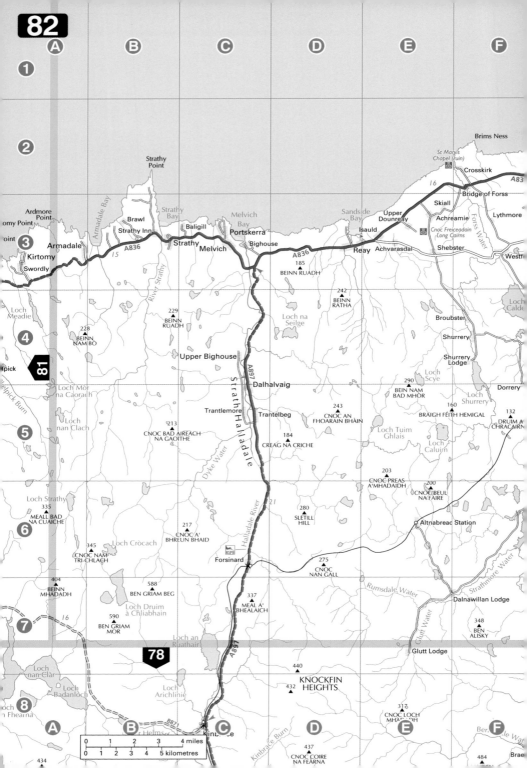

A   B   C   D   E   F

1

2

Brims Ness

St Mary's
Chapel (ruin)
Crosskirk

16   A83

Strathy
Point

Skiall
Bridge of Forss
Achreamie   Lythmore

Ardmore
Point

Melvich
Bay

Sandside
Bay   Upper
Dounreay

omy Point

Brawl

Armadale Bay

Strathy Inn   Baligill   Portskerra

Cnoc Freiceadain
Long Cairns   Forss Water

Point

3   Armadale
Kirtomy   Strathy   Melvich   Bighouse   A836   Reay
Isauld   Achvarasdal
Shebster   Westf

Swordly

River Strathy

185
BEINN RUADH

A836
Achvarasdal

242
BEINN
RATHA

Broubster   Loch
Calde

Loch
Meadie

228
BEINN
NAM BO

229
BEINN
RUADH

Loch na
Seilge

Shurrery

Shurrery
Lodge

4

81

pick

Upper Bighouse

290
BEIN NAM
BAD MHOR

Loch
Scye
Loch
Shurrery   Dorrery

Loch Mor
na Caorach

Dalhalvaig

A897

160
BRAIGH FÉITH HEMIGAL

132
DRUIM A
CHRACAIRN

Loch
nan Clach

Trantlemore

Strath Halladale

Trantelbeg

243
CNOC AN
FHOARAIN BHÀIN

184
CREAG NA CRICHE

Loch Tuim
Ghlais

5

213
CNOC BAD AIREACH
NA GAOITHE

Dyke Water

Loch
Caluim

203
CNOC PREAS
A'MHADAIDH

200
CNOC BEUL
NA FAIRE

Loch Strathy

335
MEALL BAD
NA CUAICHE

217
CNOC A'
BHREUN BHAID

21

280
SLETILL
HILL

Altnabreac Station

6

elpick Burn

345
CNOC NAM
TRI-CHLACH

Loch Cròcach

Halladale River

Forsinard

275
CNOC
NAN GALL

Dalnawillan Lodge

404
BEINN
MHADADH

588
BEN GRIAM BEG

Loch Druim
à Chliabhain

337
MEAL A'
BHEALAICH

348
BEN
ALISKY

7

16

590
BEN GRIAM
MOR

Loch an
Ruathair

A897

Glutt Water   Strathmore Water

Glutt Lodge

78

Loch
nan Clar

Loch
Badanloch

B871

Loch
Arichlinie

KinB dge

440

KNOCKFIN
HEIGHTS

Rumsdale Water

8

Loch
Fheara

432

31
CNOC LOCH
MHA DH

A897

Kinbra Burn

Ber
le Wa

Brae

A   B   C   D   E   F

0   1   2   3   4 miles
0   1   2   3   4   5 kilometres

434

437
CNOC COIRE
NA FEARNA

484

Western Isles

0 — 5 — 10 miles

0 — 5 — 10 kilometres

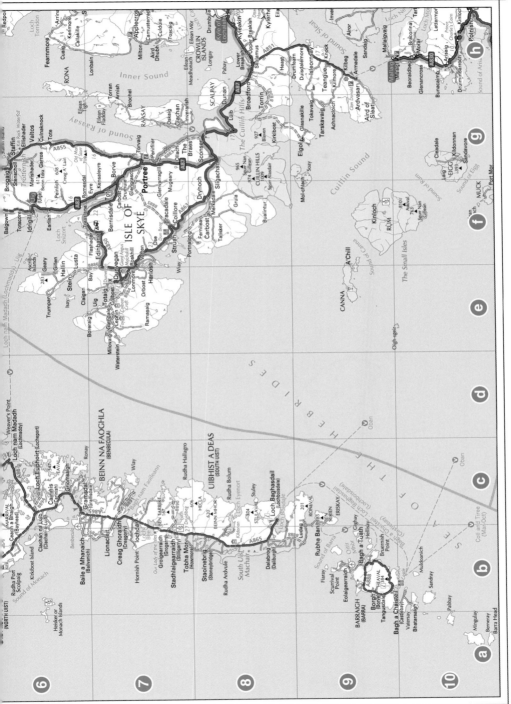

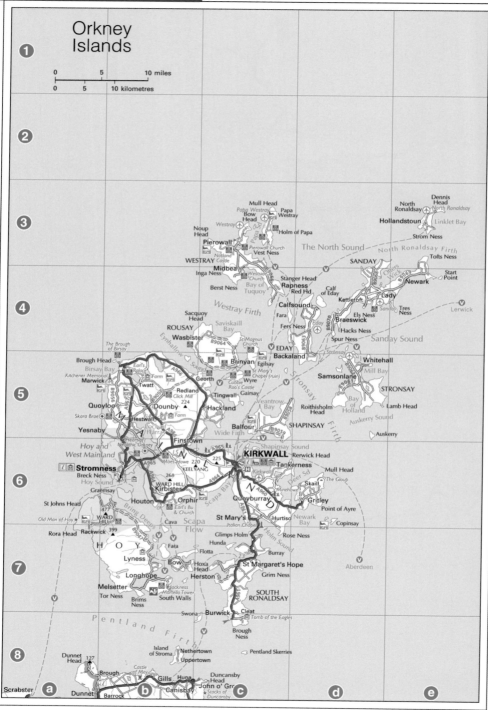

Orkney Islands

0 — 5 — 10 miles
0 — 5 — 10 kilometres

Mull Head
Papa Westray
Bow Head
Holm of Papa
Noup Head
Pierowall Church
Vest Ness
Pierowall
Notland Castle
WESTRAY
Midbea
Inga Ness
Westside Church
Stanger Head
Red Hd
Rapness
Berst Ness
Bay of Tuquoy
Calfsound
Calf of Eday
Calfsound
Fara
Fers Ness
Sacquoy Head
ROUSAY
Saviskaill Bay
St Magnus Church
Wasbister
B9064
Brinyan
Egilsay
The Brough of Birsay
Eynhallow Sound
St Mary's Chapel (ruin)
EDAY
Backaland
Brough Head
Earl's Palace
Birsay Bay
Cubbie Roo's Castle
Kitchener Memorial
Marwick
Twatt
Georth
Wyre
Gairsay
Whitehall
Mill Bay
Quoyloo
Redland
Click Mill
224
Tingwall
Samsonlane
STRONSAY
Skara Brae
Dounby
Farm
Hackland
Bay of Holland
Yesnaby
Hestwall
Lamb Head
Loch of Harray
Balfour
SHAPINSAY
Roithisholm Head
Finstown
Wide Firth
Auskerry Sound
Hoy and West Mainland
Heddle
Shapinsay Sound
Auskerry
Moel Howe 220
225
Stromness
A965
KEELYLANG
KIRKWALL
Rerwick Head
Breck Ness
268
Tankerness
Mull Head
Hoy Sound
WARD HILL
Kirbister
Minehowe
Skaill
The Gloup
Graemsay
Houton
Orphir
Quoyburray
Gritley
St Johns Head
Earl's Bu & Church
Point of Ayre
Old Man of Hoy
WARD HILL 399
Scapa Flow
St Mary's
Hurtiso
Copinsay
Rora Head
Rackwick
Cava
Italian Chapel
Rose Ness
Fara
Glimps Holm
H O Y
Flotta
Hunda
Burray
Lyness
Bow
Hoxa Head
Longhope
Herston
St Margaret's Hope
Grim Ness
Melsetter
Hackness
SOUTH RONALDSAY
Tor Ness
Martello Tower
Brims Ness
South Walls
Swona
Burwick
Cleat
Tomb of the Eagles
Pentland Firth
Brough Ness
Dunnet Head 127
Island of Stroma
Nethertown
Pentland Skerries
Brough
Castle of Mey
Uppertown
Scrabster
Dunnet
Barrock
Gills
Canisbay
Huna
John o' Gro
Duncansby Head
Stacks of Duncansby

Dennis Head
North Ronaldsay
Hollandstoun
Linklet Bay
Strom Ness
The North Sound
North Ronaldsay Firth
Tofts Ness
SANDAY
Start Point
Newark
Lerwick
Kettletoft
Lady
Els Ness
Tres Ness
Braeswick
Hacks Ness
Spur Ness
Sanday Sound
Aberdeen

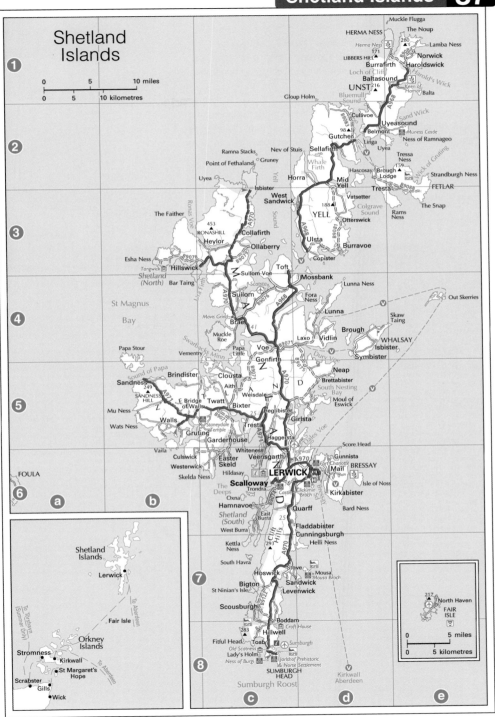

Shetland Islands

0 5 10 miles
0 5 10 kilometres

Muckle Flugga
HERMA NESS
The Noup
Herma Ness
280
LIBBERS HILL
171
Lamba Ness
Burrafirth
Norwick
Loch of Cliff
Haroldswick
Baltasound
UNST 216
Keen of
Balta
Hamar
Gloup Holm
Bluemull
Sound
Sand Wick
Cullivoe
Uyeasound
Belmont
Muness Castle
Gutcher
Ness of Ramnageo
Linga
Ramna Stacks
Nev of Stuis
Sellafirth
Uyea
Point of Fethaland
Gruney
Tressa
Ness
159
Whale
Hascosay
Brough
Uyea
Horra
Firth
Lodge
Strandburgh Ness
Isbister
Mid
FETLAR
West
Yell
Tresta
Sandwick
B9088
The Faither
Vatsetter
The Snap
188
Colgrave
RONASHILL
YELL
Sound
Rams
453
Collafirth
Ness
Heylor
Otterswick
Ollaberry
Esha Ness
Ulsta
Burravoe
Tangwick
Hillswick
Sullom Voe
Toft
Copister
Shetland
Bar Taing
Sullom Voe
Mossbank
Lunna Ness
(North)
Scatsta
Fora
St Magnus
Mavis Grind
Ness
Lunna
Out Skerries
Bay
Brae
41
Laxo
Vidlin
Brough
Skaw
Muckle
Taing
Roe
Papa
Voe
WHALSAY
Vementry
Little
Gonfirth
Isbister
Papa Stour
Neap
Symbister
Brindister
Clousta
Brettabister
Sandness
Aith
Moul of
249
Weisdale
South Nesting
Eswick
SANDNESS
E Bridge
Twatt
Bay
HILL
of Walls
Bixter
Mu Ness
Gruting
Tresta
Girlsta
Walls
Wats Ness
Haggersta
Score Head
Garderhouse
Whiteness
Gunnista
Vaila
Culswick
Veensgarth
BRESSAY
Easter
Mail
Westerwick
Skeld
Isle of Noss
FOULA
Hildasay
LERWICK
Skelda Ness
Scalloway
Kirkabister
The
Oxna
Trondra
Clickimin
Deeps
Castle
Broch
Bard Ness
Hamnavoe
Quarff
East
Shetland
Burra
Fladdabister
(South)
West Burra
Cunningsburgh
Kettla
Helli Ness
Ness
Clift
South Havra
Hills
293
Stove
Mousa
Hoswick
Sandwick
Mousa Broch
Bigton
Levenwick
St Ninian's Isle
Scousburgh
Boddam
Croft House
283
Hillwell
Fitful Head
Toab
Sumburgh
RSPB
Old Scatness
Lady's Holm
Jarlshof Prehistoric
Ness of Burgi
& Norse Settlement
SUMBURGH
HEAD
Sumburgh Roost

Shetland
Islands

Lerwick

To Toftshvn
(Summer Only)

To Aberdeen

Fair Isle

Orkney
Islands

Stromness
Kirkwall
St Margaret's
Hope
Scrabster
Gills
Wick

North Haven
217
FAIR
ISLE

0 5 miles
0 5 kilometres

Kirkwall
Aberdeen

Mileage chart

The mileage chart shows distances in miles between two towns along AA-recommended routes. Using motorways and other main roads this is normally the fastest route, though not necessarily the shortest.

The journey times, shown in hours and minutes, are average off-peak driving times along AA-recommended routes. These times should be used as a guide only and do not allow for unforeseen traffic delays, rest breaks or fuel stops.

For example, the 378 miles (608 km) journey between Glasgow and Norwich should take approximately 7 hours 28 minutes.

Journey times

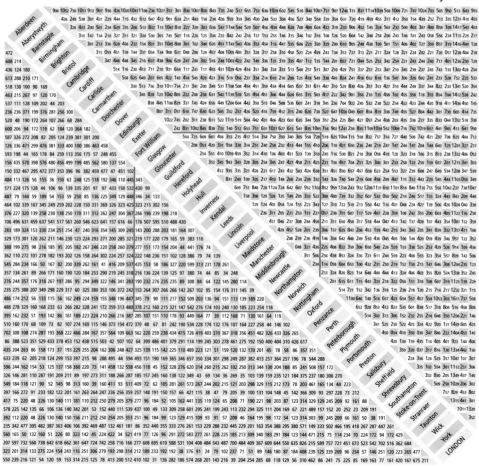

Distances in miles (one mile equals 1.6093 km)

This index lists places appearing in the main-map section of the atlas in alphabetical order. The reference following each name gives the atlas page number and grid reference of the square in which the place appears. The map shows counties, unitary authorities and administrative areas, together with a list of the abbreviated name forms used in the index. The top places of tourist interest are indexed in **red,** World Heritage sites in **green,** motorway service areas in **blue,** airports in blue *italic* and National Parks in green *italic*.

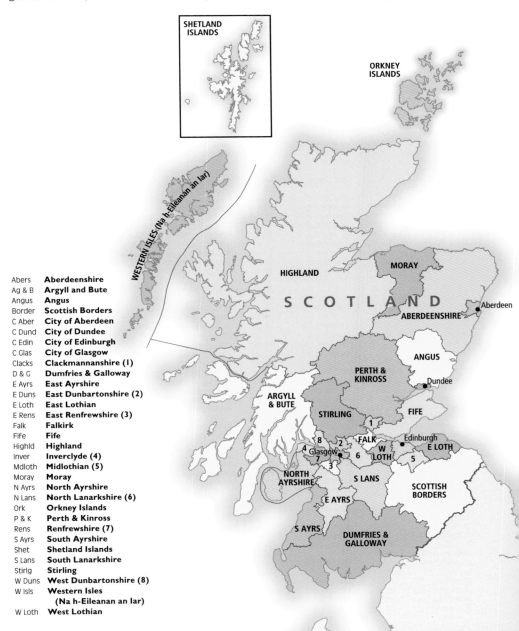

Abers	**Aberdeenshire**
Ag & B	**Argyll and Bute**
Angus	**Angus**
Border	**Scottish Borders**
C Aber	**City of Aberdeen**
C Dund	**City of Dundee**
C Edin	**City of Edinburgh**
C Glas	**City of Glasgow**
Clacks	**Clackmannanshire (1)**
D & G	**Dumfries & Galloway**
E Ayrs	**East Ayrshire**
E Duns	**East Dunbartonshire (2)**
E Loth	**East Lothian**
E Rens	**East Renfrewshire (3)**
Falk	**Falkirk**
Fife	**Fife**
Highld	**Highland**
Inver	**Inverclyde (4)**
Mdloth	**Midlothian (5)**
Moray	**Moray**
N Ayrs	**North Ayrshire**
N Lans	**North Lanarkshire (6)**
Ork	**Orkney Islands**
P & K	**Perth & Kinross**
Rens	**Renfrewshire (7)**
S Ayrs	**South Ayrshire**
Shet	**Shetland Islands**
S Lans	**South Lanarkshire**
Stirlg	**Stirling**
W Duns	**West Dunbartonshire (8)**
W Isls	**Western Isles**
	(Na h-Eileanan an Iar)
W Loth	**West Lothian**

A

Abbey St Bathans
  Border.................30 F6
Abbotrule Border....19 J6
Abbots Deuglie
  P & K...................38 B5
Aberarder Highld.....54 F1
Aberargie P & K.......38 B4
Aberchalder
  Lodge Highld........54 B5
Aberchirder Abers....68 C4
Aberdalgie P & K.....37 M4
Aberdeen C Aber......59 H4
Aberdeen Airport
  C Aber.................59 G3
Aberdeen
  Crematorium
  C Aber.................59 G4
Aberdour Fife..........29 G2
Aberfeldy P & K.......46 D6
Aberfoyle Stirlg........36 C7
Aberlady E Loth.......30 B3
Aberlemno Angus....48 E5
Aberlour Moray........67 G5
Abernethy P & K.......38 C4
Abernyte P & K........38 D2
Aberuthven P & K.....37 K4
Abington S Lans.......17 H5
Abington Services
  S Lans.................57 H4
Aboyne Abers...........57 L5
Abriachan Highld.....64 E7
Abronhill N Lans......27 K3
Acha Ag & B.............40 F5
Achahoish Ag & B....24 D3
Achalader P & K.......47 H7
Achaleven Highld....34 D1
Acha Mor W Isls.......84 f3
Achanalt Highld........63 K3
Achandunie Highld...74 E6
Achany Highld..........74 D2
Acharacle Highld......42 D3
Acharn Highld..........42 E6
Acharn P & K............46 B7
Achavanich Highld...83 H6
Achduart Highld.......76 C7
Achfary Highld..........80 D7
A'Chill Highld............50 D4
Achiltibuie Highld....76 C6
Achina Highld...........81 L4
Achinhoan Ag & B....13 J6
Achintee Highld........62 E6
Achintraid Highld.....62 C4
Achmelvich Highld...76 C4
Achmore Highld........62 D7
Achmore W Isls........84 f3
Achnacarnin
  Highld.................76 C3
Achnacarry Highld...53 J7
Achnacloich
  Highld.................51 J4
Achnaconeran
  Highld.................54 C2
Achnacroish
  Ag & B.................43 G7
Achnadrish House
  Ag & B.................41 L6
Achnafauld P & K....37 J1
Achnagarron
  Highld.................74 F7
Achnaha Highld........41 J3
Achnahaird Highld...76 B5
Achnairn Highld.......77 L6
Achnalea Highld.......43 G4

Achnamara Ag & B...24 D2
Achnasheen
  Highld.................63 J3
Achnashellach
  Lodge Highld.......62 F5
Achnastank Moray....67 G7
Achosnich Highld......41 K3
Achranich Highld......42 E6
Achreamie Highld....82 E3
Achriabhach
  Highld.................44 B3
Achriesgill Highld.....80 C5
Achtoty Highld..........81 K3
Achvaich Highld........74 F3
Achvarasdal
  Highld.................82 E3
Ackergill Highld........83 L5
Addiewell W Loth.....28 D5
Advie Highld.............66 D7
Ae D & G..................9 H4
Ae Bridgend D & G...9 H5
Affleck Abers............68 B6
Affric Lodge
  Highld.................53 J2
Ainville W Loth.........28 F5
Aird Ag & B..............33 M7
Aird D & G................2 D3
Aird W Isls...............84 g2
Aird a Mhulaidh
  W Isls..................84 e3
Aird Asaig W Isls......84 e4
Aird Dhubh Highld...61 L6
Airdeny Ag & B.........34 E2
Aird of Kinloch
  Ag & B.................33 H2
Aird of Sleat
  Highld.................51 J5
Airdrie N Lans..........27 K5
Airdriehill N Lans.....27 K5
Airds of Kells
  D & G..................8 B7
Aird Uig W Isls.........84 d2
Airidh a bhruaich
  W Isls..................84 e3
Airieland D & G........4 D4
Airlie Angus.............47 L6
Airntully P & K.........38 A1
Airor Highld.............51 L4
Airth Falk................28 B2
Aith Shet................87 C5
Alcaig Highld...........64 E3
Aldclune P & K.........46 E4
Aldivalloch Moray....57 H1
Aldochlay Ag & B.....26 C1
Aldunie Moray..........67 H8
Alexandria W Duns..26 D3
Alford Abers.............58 B3
Allanaquoich
  Abers..................56 D6
Allanbank N Lans.....27 L6
Allanton Border........31 H7
Allanton N Lans........27 L6
Allanton S Lans........27 K7
Allerton Highld.........65 H2
Alligin Shuas
  Highld.................62 C3
Alloa Clacks............37 J8
Alloway S Ayrs.........15 J5
Alltchaorunn
  Highld.................44 C6
Almondbank P & K...37 M3
Alness Highld...........74 E7
Altandhu Highld.......76 B6
Altass Highld...........74 C2
Altcreich Ag & B.......42 D8
Altgaltraig Ag & B....25 H4

Altnabreac
  Station Highld.....82 E6
Altnaharra Highld....77 M2
Altskeith Hotel
  Stirlg...................36 B6
Alva Clacks..............37 J7
Alves Moray.............66 E3
Alyth P & K..............47 K6
Amhuinnsuidhe
  W Isls..................84 d4
Amisfield Town
  D & G..................9 H5
Amulree P & K..........37 J1
Anaheilt Highld........43 G4
Ancrum Border........19 K4
Ankerville Highld......75 H6
Annan D & G...........5 L2
Annandale Water
  Services D & G.....9 J4
Annat Highld...........62 D4
Annathill N Lans......27 J4
Annbank S Ayrs.......15 K5
Anniesland C Glas....26 F5
Anstruther Fife........39 J6
An t-Ob W Isls..........84 d5
Antonine Wall Falk...27 L3
Anwoth D & G..........3 M4
Appin Ag & B...........43 J6
Applecross Highld....61 L5
Applegarth Town
  D & G..................9 J5
Appletreehall
  Border.................19 H6
Arabella Highld........75 H6
Arbirlot Angus.........48 F7
Arboll Highld...........75 J5
Arbroath Angus.......49 G7
Arbuthnott Abers....49 K2
Archencarroch
  W Duns................26 D3
Archiestown
  Moray..................66 F5
Ardallie Abers..........69 J6
Ardanaiseig Hotel
  Ag & B.................34 F3
Ardaneaskan
  Highld.................62 C7
Ardarroch Highld.....62 C6
Ardbeg Ag & B.........12 D1
Ardbeg Ag & B.........25 J5
Ardbeg Ag & B.........25 K2
Ardcharnich
  Highld.................72 F4
Ardchiavaig
  Ag & B.................32 E4
Ardchonnel Ag & B..34 D5
Ardchullarie More
  Stirlg...................36 D5
Arddarroch Ag & B..35 J7
Ardechive Highld.....53 H7
Ardeer N Ayrs..........15 H2
Ardelve Highld.........62 D8
Arden Ag & B...........26 C2
Ardentallen
  Ag & B.................34 B3
Ardentinny Ag & B...25 L2
Ardentraive
  Ag & B.................25 H4
Ardeonaig Stirlg......36 E1
Ardersier Highld......65 J4
Ardessie Highld.......72 D4
Ardfern Ag & B........34 A6
Ardfernal Ag & B......23 K4
Ardgay Highld..........74 D4
Ardgour Highld........43 K4
Ardgowan Inver.......25 L4

Ardhallow Ag & B......25 K4
Ardhasig W Isls........84 e4
Ardheslaig Highld.....62 B3
Ardindrean Highld....72 F4
Ardlamont Ag & B.....25 G5
Ardler P & K.............47 L7
Ardlui Ag & B...........35 K4
Ardlussa Ag & B.......24 B2
Ardmair Highld........72 E2
Ardmaleish Ag & B...25 J5
Ardminish Ag & B.....24 B8
Ardmolich Highld.....42 E3
Ardmore Ag & B.......26 C3
Ardmore Highld........74 F4
Ardnadam Ag & B....25 K3
Ardnagrask Highld...64 E6
Ardnarff Highld........62 D7
Ardnastang Highld...42 F4
Ardpatrick Ag & B....24 C6
Ardrishaig Ag & B....24 E2
Ardross Highld.........74 E6
Ardrossan N Ayrs.....15 G2
Ardslignish Highld...42 B4
Ardtalla Ag & B........23 J7
Ardtoe Highld..........42 C3
Arduaine Ag & B......34 A5
Ardullie Highld.........64 E2
Ardvasar Highld.......51 K5
Ardvorlich P & K......36 D3
Ardvourlie W Isls.....84 e3
Ardwell D & G..........2 D5
Arevegaig Highld.....42 D3
Argyll Forest Park
  Ag & B.................35 J6
Aribruach W Isls......84 e3
Aridhglas Ag & B......32 D3
Arileod Ag & B.........40 F5
Arinagour Ag & B.....41 G5
Ariogan Ag & B........34 C3
Arisaig Highld.........51 K7
Arisaig House
  Highld.................51 L7
Arkleton D & G........10 C4
Armadale Highld......51 K5
Armadale Highld......82 A3
Armadale W Loth.....28 C5
Arnabost Ag & B......40 F4
Arncroach Fife.........39 H6
Arndilly House
  Moray..................67 G5
Arngask P & K.........38 B5
Arnisdale Highld......52 C3
Arnish Highld..........61 J5
Arniston Mdloth......29 K6
Arnol W Isls.............84 f1
Arnprior Stirlg.........36 D7
Aros Ag & B.............42 B7
Arran N Ayrs...........14 B3
Arrina Highld...........62 B3
Arrochar Ag & B......35 K6
Artafallie Highld......64 F4
Arthrath Abers........69 H6
Artrochie Abers.......69 J7
Ascog Ag & B..........25 J5
Ashfield Stirlg.........37 G6
Ashgill S Lans.........27 K7
Ashkirk Border........19 G5
Ashton Inver...........25 L3
Asknish Ag & B.......24 F1
Astle Highld............75 G3
Athelstaneford
  E Loth.................30 C3
Attadale Highld.......62 E6
Auchbreck Moray....66 F8
Auchedly Abers.......69 G7
Auchenblae Abers...49 H1

Auchenbowie
Stirlg 27 L2
Auchencairn D & G....4 D5
Auchencairn D & G....9 G5
Auchencairn
N Ayrs.................14 D4
Auchencrow
Border 31 H6
Auchendinny
Mdloth 29 H6
Auchengray S Lans ..28 D7
Auchenhalrig
Moray 67 J3
Auchenheath
S Lans 16 F2
Auchenhessnane
D & G...................8 E3
Auchenlochan
Ag & B 25 G4
Auchenmade
N Ayrs 26 C8
Auchenmalg D & G 2 F4
Auchentiber
N Ayrs 26 C8
Auchindrain
Ag & B 34 E6
Auchindrean
Highld..................73 G5
Auchininna Abers ...68 C5
Auchinleck E Ayrs....16 B5
Auchinloch N Lans ...27 H4
Auchinstarry
N Lans 27 J3
Auchintore Highld ...43 L2
Auchiries Abers 69 K6
Auchlean Highld.......55 K5
Auchlee Abers..........59 G6
Auchleven Abers.....58 C1
Auchlochan S Lans...16 F3
Auchlossan Abers ...58 B5
Auchlyne Stirlg 36 B2
Auchmillan E Ayrs ...16 A4
Auchmithie Angus ...49 G7
Auchmuirbridge
Fife 38 C6
Auchnacree Angus ..48 D4
Auchnagatt Abers...69 H6
Auchnarrow
Moray 56 F2
Auchnotteroch
D & G...................2 B3
Auchroisk Moray 67 H4
Auchterarder
P & K...................37 K5
Auchteraw Highld ...54 B4
Auchterblair
Highld..................55 L2
Auchtercairn
Highld..................71 J6
Auchterderran
Fife 38 C7
Auchterhouse
Angus.................48 B8
Auchterless Abers...68 D6
Auchtermuchty
Fife 38 D5
Auchterneed
Highld..................64 D3
Auchtertool Fife 29 H1
Auchtertyre
Highld..................62 C8
Auchtubh Stirlg 36 C4
Auckengill Highld....83 L3
Auldearn Highld.......65 L4
Auldgirth D & G........8 F5
Auldhouse S Lans ...27 H7

Ault a' chruinn
Highld..................52 E2
Aultbea Highld..........71 K4
Aultgrishin Highld....71 H4
Aultguish Inn
Highld..................73 J7
Aultmore Moray 67 J4
Aultnagoire Highld ..54 E2
Aultnamain Inn
Highld..................74 F5
Aviemore Highld......55 L3
Avoch Highld.............65 G4
Avonbridge Falk 28 B4
Ayr S Ayrs 15 J5
Ayton Border 31 J6

B

Backaland Ork 86 d4
Backfolds Abers 69 J4
Backies Highld 75 H2
Back of Keppoch
Highld..................51 K7
Badachro Highld 71 J6
Badcall Highld..........80 B7
Badcall Highld..........80 C4
Badcaul Highld 72 D3
Baddidarrach
Highld..................76 D4
Baddinsgill Border ...28 F7
Badenscoth Abers ...68 D6
Badentarbet
Highld..................76 B6
Badenyon Abers......57 H2
Badicaul Highld 62 B8
Badlieu Border.........17 K5
Badlipster Highld 83 J5
Badluarach Highld ...72 C3
Badninish Highld......75 G3
Badrallach Highld.....72 D3
Bagh a Chaisteil
W Isls..................85 b9
Bagh a Tuath
W Isls..................85 b9
Baile Ailein W Isls....84 f3
Baile a Mhanaich
W Isls..................85 b6
Baile Mor Ag & B.....32 D3
Baillieston C Glas 27 J5
Bainshole Abers 68 B7
Baintown Fife..........38 F6
Bairnkine Border.....19 K6
Balallan W Isls.........84 f3
Balbeg Highld 64 C7
Balbeggie P & K.......38 C2
Balblair Highld 64 D5
Balblair Highld 65 G2
Balcary D & G...........4 E5
Balchraggan
Highld..................64 E5
Balchreick Highld 80 B4
Balcomie Links
Fife 39 K5
Baldinnie Fife 39 G5
Baldinnies P & K.......37 L4
Baldovie C Dund.......39 G2
Baledgarno P & K.....38 D2
Balemartine
Ag & B 40 C7
Balerno C Edin 29 G5
Balfarg Fife 38 D6
Balfield Angus 48 E3
Balfour Ork 86 c5
Balfron Stirlg............26 F1
Balgaveny Abers 68 C6

Balgonar Fife...........37 L8
Balgowan D & G.......2 D6
Balgowan Highld......54 F6
Balgown Highld........70 B7
Balgracie D & G.........2 B3
Balgray S Lans.........17 H5
Balhary P & K...........47 L6
Balholmie P & K.......38 B1
Baligill Highld...........82 C3
Balintore Angus 47 L5
Balintore Highld 75 J6
Balintraid Highld 75 G7
Balivanich W Isls.....85 b6
Balkeerie Angus 48 B7
Ballachulish Highld ...43 L5
Ballanlay Ag & B 25 H6
Ballantrae S Ayrs......6 C5
Ballater Abers 57 J6
Ballchraggan
Highld..................75 G6
Ballencrieff E Loth ...30 B3
Ballevullin Ag & B.....40 B6
Balliekine N Ayrs......13 L2
Balliemore Ag & B....34 F7
Balligmorrie S Ayrs....6 F4
Ballimore Stirlg.........36 C4
Ballindalloch
Moray 66 E6
Ballindean P & K.......38 D2
Ballingry Fife 38 C7
Ballinluig P & K.........46 F6
Ballinshoe Angus 48 C5
Ballintuim P & K........47 H5
Balloch Highld..........65 H5
Balloch N Lans 27 K4
Balloch P & K 37 H4
Balloch S Ayrs...........7 G3
Balloch W Duns.........26 D3
Ballygown Ag & B....41 K7
Ballygrant Ag & B 23 G5
Ballyhaugh Ag & B....40 F5
Balmaclellan D & G....8 B6
Balmae D & G............4 C6
Balmaha Stirlg.........26 D1
Balmalcolm Fife.......38 E5
Balmangan D & G......4 B5
Balmedie Abers 59 H2
Balmerino Fife 38 F3
Balmichael N Ayrs....14 B3
Balmore E Duns........27 G4
Balmuchy Highld.......75 J5
Balmule Fife 29 G2
Balmullo Fife 39 G4
Balnacoil Lodge
Highld..................78 E6
Balnacra Highld 62 F5
Balnacroft Abers......57 G6
Balnafoich Highld 65 G7
Balnaguard P & K.....46 E6
Balnahard Ag & B 32 F1
Balnahard Ag & B 32 F7
Balnain Highld 64 C7
Balnakeil Highld 80 F2
Balquharn P & K.......37 L1
Balquhidder Stirlg.....36 C3
Baltasound Shet.......87 e1
Baltersan D & G.........3 J3
Balvicar Ag & B.........33 M4
Balvraid Highld 52 C3
Balvraid Highld 65 K7
Banavie Highld 43 L2
Banchory Abers........58 D6
Banchory-
Devenick Abers ...59 G5
Bandirran P & K........38 C2
Banff Abers 68 D2

Bankend D & G 5 H2
Bankfoot P & K.........37 M1
Bankglen E Ayrs.......16 C6
Bankhead C Aber 59 G4
Bankhead S Lans.....17 J1
Banknock Falk..........27 K3
Bankshill D & G 9 L5
Bannockburn
Stirlg...................27 L1
Banton N Lans..........27 K3
Barabhas W Isls.......84 f1
Barassie S Ayrs........15 J3
Barbaraville
Highld..................75 G6
Barbieston S Ayrs.....15 K5
Barcaldine Ag & B 43 J7
Bardowie E Duns......27 G4
Bardrainney Inver.....26 C4
Barfad D & G..............3 G2
Bargeddie N Lans.....27 J5
Bargrennan D & G......7 H6
Barlanark C Glas......27 H5
Barlochan D & G.......4 C3
Barmollack Ag & B....13 K1
Barnacarry Ag & B ...34 E8
Barnbarroch D & G.....4 E4
Barncorkrie D & G......2 D7
Barnhead Angus 49 G5
Barnhill C Dund 39 H2
Barnhill Moray 66 E3
Barnhills D & G..........6 B7
Barnton C Edin 29 G4
Barr S Ayrs.................7 G4
Barra W Isls..............85 b9
Barra Airport W Isls..85 b9
Barrachan D & G........3 H5
Barraigh W Isls.........85 b9
Barrapoll Ag & B 40 B7
Barrhead E Rens.......26 F6
Barrhill S Ayrs............6 F5
Barrmill N Ayrs.........26 C7
Barrock Highld..........83 J2
Barry Angus..............39 J1
Barthol Chapel
Abers..................68 F7
Barvas W Isls............84 f1
Bassendean
Border 19 K1
Bathgate W Loth 28 D5
Bathville W Loth 28 D5
Battledykes Angus ..48 D5
Baulds Abers 58 B6
Bay Highld 60 D4
Bayble W Isls............84 g2
Bayhead W Isls.........85 b6
Bearsden E Duns......26 F4
Beattock D & G..........9 J2
Beauly Highld............64 E5
Bedrule Border 19 J5
Beeswing D & G.........4 F2
Beinn Na Faoghla
W Isls..................85 c7
Beith N Ayrs..............26 C7
Belhaven E Loth 30 E3
Belhelvie Abers.........59 H2
Belhinnie Abers 67 K8
Bellabeg Abers 57 H3
Bellanoch Ag & B......34 A8
Bellaty Angus...........47 K4
Bellfield S Lans.........16 F3
Bellfield S Lans.........17 J5
Belloch Ag & B 13 H2
Bellochantuy
Ag & B 13 H3
Bellshill N Lans.........27 J6
Bellside N Lans 27 L6

Bellsquarry W Loth .. **28** E5
Belmaduthy
  Highld...............**65** G3
Belmont S Ayrs **15** J5
Belmont Shet..........**87** d2
Belnacraig Abers.......**57** J3
Belses Border...........**19** J4
Benbecula W Isls.....**85** c7
Benbecula Airport
  W Isls..................**85** c6
Benbuie D & G...........**8** C3
Benderloch Ag & B...**43** H8
Benholm Abers..........**49** K3
Benmore Ag & B........**25** K4
Bennan N Ayrs **14** C5
Ben Nevis Highld **44** B3
Benslie N Ayrs **15** J2
Benthoul C Aber.......**58** F5
Bentpath D & G **10** B4
Benvie Angus............**38** E2
Beoraidbeg Highld...**51** L6
Bernera Highld **52** C2
Bernisdale Highld......**60** F4
Berriedale Highld **79** K4
Berryhillock Moray....**67** L3
Berryhillock Moray ...**67** L4
Bettyhill Highld..........**81** L3
Bhaltos W Isls.........**84** d2
Bhatarsaigh W Isls..**85** b10
Bieldside C Aber **59** G5
Big Balcraig D & G....**3** H6
Big Carlae D & G **8** B3
Biggar S Lans............**17** K2
Bigholms D & G.........**10** B6
Bighouse Highld.......**82** C3
Big Sand Highld **71** H5
Bigton Shet..............**87** c7
Bilbster Highld..........**83** K5
Bilston Mdloth..........**29** H5
Binniehill Falk **28** B4
Birgham Border.........**20** B2
Birichin Highld **75** G3
Birkenbog Abers **67** L2
Birkenhills Abers.......**68** E5
Birkhall Abers **57** H6
Birkhill Angus............**38** F1
Birkhill D & G **18** B6
Birnam P & K.............**47** G7
Birness Abers............**69** J7
Birse Abers...............**58** B6
Birsemore Abers.......**57** L5
Bishopbriggs
  E Duns..................**27** G4
Bishopmill Moray......**66** F2
Bishopton Rens........**26** E4
Bixter Shet...............**87** c5
Blackadder Border....**31** H7
Blackburn Abers........**58** F3
Blackburn W Loth **28** D5
Blackcraig E Ayrs **16** C7
Black Crofts
  Ag & B **34** D1
Blackdog Abers **59** H3
Blackford P & K **17** J5
Blackhall C Edin.......**29** G4
Blackhaugh
  Border...................**18** F2
Blackhill Abers..........**69** K3
Blackhill Abers...........**69** K5
Blackhill of
  Clackriach
  Abers....................**69** H5
Blacklaw D & G **17** K7
Blacklunans P & K....**47** J4
Blackness Falk **28** E3
Blackridge W Loth....**28** B5

Blacksboat Moray **66** E6
Blackshaw D & G.......**5** J2
Blacktop C Aber **59** G4
Blackwaterfoot
  N Ayrs **14** A4
Blackwood D & G **8** F5
Blackwood S Lans ...**16** F1
Bladnoch D & G **3** J4
Blaich Highld.............**43** K2
Blain Highld...............**42** D3
Blair Atholl P & K......**46** D4
Blair Drummond
  Stirlg....................**36** F7
Blairgowrie P & K....**47** J7
Blairhall Fife.............**28** D2
Blairingone P & K....**37** K7
Blairlogie Stirlg........**37** H7
Blairmore Ag & B.....**25** L2
Blairmore Highld......**80** C4
Blair's Ferry
  Ag & B **25** G4
Blanefield Stirlg.......**26** F3
Blantyre S Lans........**27** J6
Blar a' Chaorainn
  Highld...................**43** L3
Blargie Highld **54** F6
Blarmachfoldach
  Highld...................**43** L3
Blawquhairn D & G...**8** B5
Blebocraigs Fife......**39** G4
Blegbie E Loth..........**30** B6
Bloomfield Border ...**19** J4
Blyth Bridge
  Border...................**17** M1
Blythe Border **30** D7
Boarhills Fife...........**39** J5
Boath Highld **74** D6
Boat of Garten
  Highld...................**55** L2
Boddam Abers.........**69** L6
Boddam Shet...........**87** c7
Bogallan Highld.......**64** F4
Bogbrae Abers.........**69** J7
Bogend S Ayrs.........**15** K3
Boggs Holdings
  E Loth...................**29** L4
Boghall Mdloth........**29** H5
Boghall W Loth **28** D5
Boghead S Lans **16** F2
Bogmoor Moray.......**67** H2
Bogmuir Abers **49** G3
Bogniebrae Abers....**68** B5
Bogroy Highld..........**55** L2
Bogue D & G.............**8** B6
Bohuntine Highld.....**53** L8
Bolshan Angus.........**49** G6
Boltenstone Abers....**57** J3
Bolton E Loth **30** B4
Bonar Bridge
  Highld...................**74** E3
Bonawe Ag & B.......**34** E2
Bonchester
  Bridge Border........**19** J6
Bo'ness Falk............**28** D3
Bonhill W Duns.......**26** D3
Bonjedward
  Border...................**19** K5
Bonkle N Lans **27** L6
Bonnington Angus ..**48** F7
Bonnybank Fife........**38** F6
Bonnybridge Falk.....**27** L3
Bonnykelly Abers.....**69** G4
Bonnyrigg Mdloth....**29** J5
Bonnyton Angus......**48** B8
Bonshaw Tower
  D & G....................**9** M7

Boon Border..............**19** J1
Borders
  Crematorium
  Border...................**19** H3
Boreland D & G **9** L4
Boreraig Highld **60** C4
Borgh W Isls.............**84** f1
Borgh W Isls.............**85** b9
Borgie Highld............**81** K4
Borgue D & G **4** B5
Borgue Highld...........**79** K4
Borneskitaig
  Highld...................**70** B7
Borness D & G...........**4** A5
Borrowstoun Falk....**28** D3
Borthwickbrae
  Border...................**18** F6
Borthwickshiels
  Border...................**18** F6
Borve Highld.............**61** G5
Borve W Isls.............**84** d4
Borve W Isls.............**84** f1
Borve W Isls.............**85** b9
Bothwell S Lans **27** J6
Bothwell Services
  S Lans...................**27** J6
Bottomcraig Fife......**38** F3
Bousd Ag & B............**41** G4
Bow Ork....................**86** b7
Bowden Border.........**19** H4
Bower Highld............**83** J3
Bowermadden
  Highld...................**83** J3
Bowershall Fife........**28** F1
Bowhouse D & G **5** H2
Bowland Border........**19** G2
Bowling W Duns.......**26** E4
Bowmore Ag & B.......**22** F6
Bow of Fife Fife........**38** E5
Bowriefauld
  Angus....................**48** E6
Boyndie Abers **68** C2
Boyndlie Abers **69** G2
Boysack Angus.........**49** G6
Brabstermire
  Highld...................**83** K2
Bracadale Highld......**60** E6
Brackenhirst
  N Lans **27** K5
Brackletter
  Highld...................**53** J8
Braco P & K..............**37** H5
Bracobrae Moray **67** L4
Bracora Highld..........**51** L6
Bracorina Highld **51** L6
Brae Highld...............**65** G2
Brae Shet.................**87** c4
Braeface Falk............**27** K3
Braehead Angus.......**49** H5
Braehead D & G.........**3** J4
Braehead S Lans **28** C7
Braemar Abers **56** E6
Braemore Highld.......**73** G5
Braemore Highld.......**79** J3
Brae Roy Lodge
  Highld...................**53** L6
Braeside Inver..........**25** L4
Braes of Coul
  Angus....................**47** L5
Braes of Enzie
  Moray...................**67** J3
Braeswick Ork **86** d4
Braevallich Ag & B ...**34** D6
Bragar W Isls............**84** f2
Braidwood S Lans **27** L8
Branault Highld........**42** B3

Branchill Moray **66** D4
Branderburgh
  Moray....................**66** F1
Brathens Abers.........**58** D5
Brawl Highld..............**82** B3
Breakachy Highld......**64** D5
Brealangwell
  Lodge Highld........**74** C3
Breanais W Isls.........**84** d3
Breascleit W Isls.......**84** e2
Breasclete W Isls......**84** e2
Brechin Angus **48** F4
Breich W Loth **28** C6
Brenfield Ag & B.......**24** E2
Brenish W Isls...........**84** d3
Bressay Shet............**87** d6
Brettabister Shet......**87** d5
Brideswell Abers.......**68** B6
Bridgend Abers **67** L7
Bridgend Ag & B.......**13** K2
Bridgend Ag & B.......**23** G6
Bridgend Angus........**48** E3
Bridgend D & G.........**17** L7
Bridgend Fife............**38** F5
Bridgend Moray.........**67** J7
Bridgend P & K.........**38** B3
Bridgend W Loth.......**28** E3
Bridgend of
  Lintrathen
  Angus....................**47** L5
Bridge of Alford
  Abers....................**58** B2
Bridge of Allan
  Stirlg....................**37** G7
Bridge of Avon
  Moray...................**56** E2
Bridge of Avon
  Moray...................**66** E7
Bridge of Balgie
  P & K **45** J6
Bridge of
  Brewlands
  Angus....................**47** J4
Bridge of Brown
  Highld...................**56** D2
Bridge of Cally
  P & K **47** J6
Bridge of Canny
  Abers....................**58** C6
Bridge of
  Craigisla Angus ...**47** K5
Bridge of Dee
  D & G.....................**4** C3
Bridge of Don
  C Aber **59** H4
Bridge of Dulsie
  Highld...................**65** L6
Bridge of Dye
  Abers....................**58** C7
Bridge of Earn
  P & K **38** B4
Bridge of Ericht
  P & K **45** H3
Bridge of Feugh
  Abers....................**58** D6
Bridge of Forss
  Highld...................**82** F2
Bridge of Gairn
  Abers....................**57** H6
Bridge of Gaur
  P & K **45** H5
Bridge of
  Marnoch Abers....**68** B4
Bridge of Orchy
  Ag & B **44** E7
Bridge of Tilt P & K ..**46** D4

Bridge of Tynet
Moray 67 J3
Bridge of Walls
Shet 87 b5
Bridge of Weir
Rens 26 D5
Brightons Falk 28 C3
Brig o'Turk Stirlg .. 36 C6
Brindister Shet 87 c5
Brinyan Ork 86 C5
Broadfield Inver 26 C4
Broadford Highld 51 K2
Broadgairhill
Border 18 C7
Broadhaugh
Border 31 H7
Broadley Moray 67 J3
Brochel Highld 61 J5
Brochroy Ag & B 34 E2
Brocketsbrae
S Lans 16 F2
Brodick N Ayrs 14 C3
Brodie Moray 66 B3
Brogaig Highld 70 C7
Brookfield Rens 26 D5
Brora Highld 78 F7
Broubster Highld 82 F4
Brough Highld 83 J2
Brough Shet 87 d4
Brough Lodge
Shet 87 d2
Broughton Border 17 L3
Broughton Mains
D & G 3 J6
Broughty Ferry
C Dund 39 H2
Brownhill Abers 69 G6
Brownhills Fife 39 H4
Broxburn E Loth 30 E4
Broxburn W Loth 28 E4
Bruan Highld 83 K7
Bruar P & K 46 C3
Brucefield Highld ... 75 K4
Bruchag Ag & B 25 J6
Bruichladdich
Ag & B 22 E6
Brunery Highld 42 E3
Brunton Fife 38 E3
Brydekirk D & G 9 L7
Bualintur Highld 50 F2
Buccleuch Border 18 E6
Buchanan Smithy
Stirlg 26 E1
Buchanhaven
Abers 69 L5
Buchanty P & K 37 J2
Buchany Stirlg 36 F6
Buchlyvie Stirlg 36 C8
Buckhaven Fife 38 F7
Buckie Moray 67 J2
Buckpool Moray 67 J2
Bucksburn C Aber 59 G4
Bulwark Abers 69 H5
Bunacaimb Highld 51 K7
Bunarkaig Highld 53 J7
Bunchrew Highld 64 F5
Bundalloch Highld ... 62 D8
Bunessan Ag & B 32 E3
Bunnahabhain
Ag & B 23 H4
Buntait Highld 64 C7
Burg Ag & B 41 J7
Burghead Moray 66 D1
Burnbrae N Lans 28 B6
Burnfoot Border 18 F6
Burnfoot Border 19 H6

Burnfoot D & G 9 G4
Burnfoot D & G 10 C3
Burnfoot P & G 10 C4
Burnfoot P & K 37 K6
Burnhaven Abers 69 L5
Burnhead D & G 8 E3
Burnhervie Abers 58 D2
Burnhouse N Ayrs 26 D7
Burnmouth
Border 31 K6
Burn of Cambus
Stirlg 36 F6
Burnside Angus 48 C4
Burnside Angus 48 E6
Burnside Fife 38 B5
Burnside Moray 66 E1
Burnside W Loth 28 E3
Burnside of
Duntrune
Angus 39 G1
Burntisland Fife 29 H2
Burrafirth Shet 87 e1
Burravoe Shet 87 d3
Burrelton P & K 47 K8
Burwick Ork 86 c8
Busby E Rens 27 G6
Bush Abers 49 J4
Bute Ag & B 25 H4
Butterdean Border ... 31 G5
Butterstone P & K ... 47 G7

C

Cabrach Ag & B 23 J5
Cabrach Moray 67 J8
Cadder E Duns 27 G4
Caddonfoot
Border 19 G3
Cadham Fife 38 D6
Caerlanrig Border ... 10 D2
Cairinis W Isls 85 c6
Cairnbaan Ag & B 24 E1
Cairnbulg Abers 69 J2
Cairncross Border ... 31 J5
Cairncurran Inver ... 26 C4
Cairndow Ag & B 35 H5
Cairneyhill Fife 28 E2
Cairngarroch
D & G 2 C5
Cairngorms
National Park 56 C5
Cairnie Abers 67 K5
Cairnorrie Abers 69 G6
Cairnryan D & G 2 C2
Cairnty Moray 67 H4
Calanais W Isls 84 e2
Calcots Moray 67 G2
Calderbank N Lans ... 27 K5
Caldercruix N Lans .. 27 L5
Caldermill S Lans ... 16 D2
Calderwood
S Lans 27 H7
Calfsound Ork 86 d4
Calgary Ag & B 41 J6
Califer Moray 66 D3
California Falk 28 B3
Callakille Highld ... 61 L4
Callander Stirlg 36 D5
Callanish W Isls 84 e2
Calligarry Highld ... 51 K5
Calvine P & K 46 C3
Calzeat Border 17 L3
Camasachoirce
Highld 42 F4
Camasine Highld 42 F4

Camas Luinie
Highld 62 E8
Camastianavaig
Highld 61 H6
Camault Muir
Highld 64 D6
Cambus Clacks 37 H8
Cambusavie
Platform Highld .. 75 G3
Cambusbarron
Stirlg 37 G8
Cambuskenneth
Stirlg 37 G8
Cambuslang
S Lans 27 H6
Cambus o' May
Abers 57 J5
Cambuswallace
S Lans 17 K2
Camelon Falk 28 B3
Camerory Highld 66 C7
Camghouran P & K 45 J5
Camieston Border 19 J4
Cammachmore
Abers 59 G6
Camore Highld 75 G4
Campbeltown
Ag & B 13 J5
Campbeltown
Airport Ag & B 13 H5
Cample D & G 8 F4
Campmuir P & K 47 K8
Camps W Loth 28 E5
Camptown Border 19 K6
Camserney P & K 46 C6
Camusnagaul
Highld 43 L2
Camusnagaul
Highld 72 D4
Camusteel Highld 61 L6
Camusterrach
Highld 61 L6
Candacraig Abers 57 H5
Candy Mill Border ... 17 L2
Canisbay Highld 83 L2
Canna Highld 50 C4
Cannich Highld 63 L7
Canonbie D & G 10 C6
Cantraywood
Highld 65 J5
Caol Highld 43 L2
Caolas Scalpaigh
W Isls 84 e4
Caoles Ag & B 40 D6
Caonich Highld 53 G6
Caplaw E Rens 26 E6
Cappercleuch
Border 18 C5
Caputh P & K 47 H7
Carbeth Inn Stirlg .. 26 F3
Carbost Highld 60 F5
Carbost Highld 60 F7
Cardenden Fife 38 C7
Cardhu Moray 66 F5
Cardrain D & G 2 D8
Cardrona Border 18 D2
Cardross Ag & B 26 C3
Cardross
Crematorium
Ag & B 26 C3
Cardryne D & G 2 D7
Careston Angus 48 E4
Carfin N Lans 27 K6
Carfraemill Border .. 30 B7
Cargenbridge
D & G 9 G6

Cargill P & K 47 J8
Carie P & K 45 K5
Carinish W Isls 85 c6
Carlabhagh W Isls ... 84 e2
Carlincraig Abers ... 68 D5
Carlops Border 29 G6
Carloway W Isls 84 e2
Carluke S Lans 27 L7
Carmacoup S Lans 16 F4
Carmichael S Lans ... 17 H2
Carmunnock
C Glas 27 G6
Carmyle C Glas 27 H6
Carmyllie Angus 48 E7
Carnbee Fife 39 J6
Carnbo P & K 37 L6
Carnbrogie Abers 68 F8
Carndu Highld 62 D8
Carnduff S Lans 16 D1
Carnell E Ayrs 15 L3
Carn-gorm Highld 52 E2
Carnie Abers 58 F4
Carnock Fife 28 E1
Carnousie Abers 68 C4
Carnoustie Angus 39 J1
Carnwath S Lans 17 J1
Carradale Ag & B 13 K2
Carrbridge Highld ... 55 L2
Carrick Ag & B 24 F2
Carrick Castle
Ag & B 35 H8
Carriden Falk 28 D3
Carrington Mdloth ... 29 J6
Carron Falk 28 B2
Carron Moray 66 F6
Carronbridge
D & G 8 F3
Carron Bridge
Stirlg 27 K2
Carronshore Falk 28 B2
Carrutherstown
D & G 9 J7
Carruth House
Inver 26 C5
Carsaig Ag & B 33 H3
Carseriggan D & G 3 G2
Carsethorn D & G 5 H3
Carskey Ag & B 13 H7
Carsluith D & G 3 K4
Carsphairn D & G 7 L4
Carstairs S Lans 17 H1
Carstairs Junction
S Lans 17 J1
Cartland S Lans 17 G1
Castlebay W Isls 85 b9
Castlecary Falk 27 K3
Castle Douglas
D & G 4 D3
Castlehill Border ... 18 C3
Castlehill Highld ... 83 H2
Castlehill W Duns ... 26 D3
Castle Kennedy
D & G 2 D3
Castle Lachlan
Ag & B 34 E7
Castlemilk C Glas ... 27 G6
Castle O'er D & G ... 10 A4
Castle Stuart
Highld 65 J5
Castleton Border 10 E4
Castletown Highld ... 83 H3
Catacol N Ayrs 24 F7
Cathcart C Glas 27 G6
Catlodge Highld 54 F6
Catrine E Ayrs 16 B4
Cattadale Ag & B 13 H7

Catterline Abers 49 L2
Cauldcots Angus 49 G6
Cauldhame Stirlg....36 E8
Cauldmill Border 19 H6
Caulkerbush D & G....5 G4
Caulside D & G 10 D6
Causeway End
D & G......................3 J3
Causewayend
S Lans 17 K3
Causewayhead
Stirlg......................37 G7
Causeyend Abers ...59 H2
Caverton Mill
Border 19 M4
Cawdor Highld.......65 K4
Ceann a Bhaigh
W Isls 85 b6
Ceannacroc
Lodge Highld 53 K3
Cearsiadar W Isls ...84 f3
Cellardyke Fife 39 J6
Ceres Fife 38 F5
Challoch D & G........3 H2
Chapel Fife 38 D8
Chapelhall N Lans ...27 K5
Chapel Hill Abers ...69 K7
Chapelhope
Border 18 C5
Chapelknowe
D & G.....................10 B7
Chapel of Garioch
Abers 58 D1
Chapel Rossan
D & G......................2 D6
Chapelton Angus 49 G6
Chapelton S Lans....27 J8
Chapeltown
Moray.....................56 F2
Charleston Angus 48 C7
Charlestown
C Aber 59 H5
Charlestown Fife ...28 E2
Charlestown
Highld.....................65 G5
Charlestown
Highld.....................71 J6
Charlottetown
Fife 38 E5
Charterhall Border...31 G8
Chartershall Stirlg....27 K1
Chatto Border 20 B5
Chesterhill Mdloth....29 K5
Chesters Border 19 J5
Chesters Border 19 K7
Cheviot Hills 20 A7
Chirnside Border 31 H6
Chirnsidebridge
Border 31 H7
Chisholme Border 18 F6
Chlenry D & G..........2 D3
Chrisswell Inver 25 L4
Clabhach Ag & B......40 F5
Clachaig Ag & B.......25 J3
Clachan Ag & B.......24 C6
Clachan Ag & B.......34 A4
Clachan Ag & B.......43 G7
Clachan Highld.......61 H6
Clachan-a-Luib
W Isls 85 c6
Clachan Mor
Ag & B 40 C6
Clachan na Luib
W Isls 85 c6
Clachan of
Campsie E Duns ..27 G3

Clachan-Seil
Ag & B 33 M4
Clachnaharry
Highld.....................65 G5
Clachtoll Highld 76 C3
Clackavoid P & K......47 J4
Clackmannan
Clacks 37 J8
Clackmarras
Moray.....................66 F3
Cladich Ag & B 34 F3
Claggan Highld 42 E6
Claigan Highld.........60 C4
Claonaig Ag & B......24 E6
Clarebrand D & G 4 D2
Clarencefield
D & G......................5 J2
Clarilaw Border.......19 H5
Clarkston E Rens 27 G6
Clashmore Highld....75 G4
Clashmore Highld....76 C3
Clashnessie Highld...76 C3
Clashnoir Moray 56 F2
Clathy P & K 37 K4
Clathymore P & K.....37 L3
Clatt Abers..............57 L1
Claygate D & G.......10 D6
Clayock Highld.........83 H4
Cleadale Highld........51 G7
Cleat Ork.................86 c8
Cleekhimin N Lans....27 K6
Cleghornie E Loth 30 D2
Cleish P & K 38 A7
Cleland N Lans 27 L6
Clenamacrie
Ag & B 34 C2
Clenerty Abers........68 E3
Cleongart Ag & B.....13 H3
Clephanton Highld...65 J4
Clerkhill D & G.........10 A3
Cleuch-head D & G....8 E3
Clinterty C Aber......58 F3
Clintmains Border ...19 J3
Clochan Moray........67 J3
Clola Abers 69 J5
Closeburn D & G 8 F4
Closeburnmill
D & G......................8 F3
Clousta Shet...........87 c5
Clova Angus 48 B2
Clovenfords
Border 19 G3
Clovulin Highld 43 K4
Cluanie Inn Highld...53 G3
Cluanie Lodge
Highld.....................53 G3
Clugston D & G 3 H4
Clunas Highld..........65 K5
Clune Highld............55 J1
Clunes Highld..........53 J7
Clunie P & K............47 H7
Cluny Fife 38 D7
Clydebank W Duns...26 F4
Clydebank
Crematorium
W Duns...................26 E4
Clynder Ag & B........26 A2
Cnoc W Isls.............84 g2
Coalburn S Lans 16 F3
Coalsnaughton
Clacks 37 J7
Coaltown of
Balgonie Fife 38 E7
Coaltown of
Wemyss Fife 38 E7
Coatbridge N Lans ...27 J5

Coatdyke N Lans 27 K5
Coburby Abers.........69 H2
Cock Bridge Abers ...57 G4
Cockburnspath
Border 31 G4
Cockenzie and
Port Seton
E Loth.....................29 L4
Coignafearn
Highld.....................55 H2
Coilacriech Abers 57 H6
Coilantogle Stirlg 36 D6
Coillore Highld 60 E6
Col W Isls................84 g2
Colaboll Highld 77 L6
Colbost Highld 60 C5
Coldbackie Highld....81 J4
Coldingham
Border 31 J5
Coldstream Border...20 C2
Coldwells Abers.......69 H6
Colenden P & K........38 B2
Colinsburgh Fife 39 H6
Colinton C Edin........29 H5
Colintraive Ag & B....25 H4
Coll Ag & B..............41 G5
Collace P & K...........38 C2
Collafirth Shet 87 c3
Coll Airport Ag & B....40 F5
College of
Roseisle Moray 66 E2
Collessie Fife..........38 E5
Collieston Abers 69 K8
Collin D & G..............9 H6
Colliston Angus.......48 F7
Colmonell S Ayrs........6 D5
Colnabaichin
Abers 57 G4
Colonsay Ag & B......32 E7
Colonsay Airport
Ag & B 32 E8
Colpy Abers 68 C7
Colquhar Border......18 E2
Coltfield Moray........66 D2
Colvend D & G..........4 F4
Comers Abers 58 D4
Compstonend
D & G......................4 B4
Comrie Fife 28 D1
Comrie P & K............37 G3
Conaglen House
Highld.....................43 K3
Conchra Highld.......62 D8
Concraigie P & K......47 H7
Condorrat N Lans 27 K4
Conheath D & G........5 H2
Conicavel Moray......66 B4
Connel Ag & B..........34 C1
Connel Park E Ayrs...16 C6
Conon Bridge
Highld.....................64 E4
Contin Highld...........64 C3
Cookney Abers 59 G6
Copister Shet...........87 d3
Cordon N Ayrs..........14 D4
Corgarff Abers.........57 G4
Cormuir Angus.........47 L3
Cornhill Abers 68 B3
Cornoigmore
Ag & B 40 C6
Corntown Highld......64 E3
Corpach Highld.........43 L2
Corrachree Abers.....57 K4
Corran Highld...........43 K4
Corran Highld...........52 C4
Corrie D & G..............9 L5

Corrie N Ayrs 14 C2
Corriecravie
N Ayrs 14 B5
Corriegills N Ayrs.....14 D3
Corriegour Lodge
Hotel Highld........53 K6
Corriemoille
Highld.....................64 B2
Corrimony Highld.....64 B7
Corrow Ag & B.........35 H7
Corry Highld 51 K1
Corsindae Abers 58 D4
Corsock D & G 8 D6
Corstorphine
C Edin.....................29 G4
Cortachy Angus.......48 C4
Coruanan Highld 43 L3
Coshieville P & K......46 C6
Cothal Abers 59 G3
Cottown Abers 58 E3
Cottown Abers 67 L8
Cottown of Gight
Abers 68 F6
Coulaghailtro
Ag & B 24 C5
Coulags Highld.........62 E5
Coull Abers 57 L5
Coulport Ag & B.......25 L2
Coulter S Lans 17 K3
Coultra Fife 38 F3
Coupar Angus
P & K......................47 K7
Cour Ag & B.............24 D8
Courteachan
Highld.....................51 L6
Cousland Mdloth 29 K5
Cove Ag & B.............25 L2
Cove Border 31 G4
Cove Highld 71 J3
Cove Bay C Aber......59 H5
Covington S Lans.....17 J2
Cowdenbeath Fife...29 G1
Cowie Stirlg.............27 L1
Coylton S Ayrs.........15 K5
Coylumbridge
Highld.....................55 L3
Craggan Highld........56 C1
Craibstone Moray.....67 L3
Craichie Angus........48 E6
Craig Angus............49 H5
Craig Highld............63 G4
Craigbank E Ayrs.....16 C6
Craigburn Border.....29 H7
Craigcleuch D & G....10 C5
Craigdam Abers.......68 F7
Craigdhu Ag & B......34 B6
Craigearn Abers 58 D3
Craigellachie
Moray.....................67 G5
Craigend P & K.........38 B24
Craigend Rens 26 E4
Craigendoran
Ag & B 26 C3
Craigends Rens 26 D5
Craighlaw D & G........3 G3
Craighouse Ag & B...23 K5
Craigie P & K 47 H7
Craigie S Ayrs.........15 K3
Craigiefold Abers 69 H2
Craigley D & G..........4 D4
Craiglockhart
C Edin.....................29 H4
Craigmillar C Edin....29 J4
Craigneston D & G 8 D5
Craigneuk N Lans 27 K5
Craigneuk N Lans 27 K6

Craignure Ag & B......42 E8
Craigo Angus 49 H4
Craigrothie Fife.......38 F5
Craigruie Stirlg.......36 B4
Craigton Angus 48 E8
Craigton C Aber.......58 F5
Craigton E Rens.......26 F7
Craigton
Crematorium
C Glas................26 F5
Craigton of Airlie
Angus..................48 B6
Crail Fife 39 K5
Crailing Border 19 L4
Cramond C Edin 29 G3
Cramond Bridge
C Edin..................29 G4
Cranshaws Border ...30 E6
Craobh Haven
Ag & B.................34 A6
Crarae Ag & B.........34 A7
Crask Inn Highld 77 L4
Crask of Aigas
Highld..................64 D6
Crathes Abers 58 E6
Crathie Abers 57 G6
Crathie Highld..........54 E6
Crawford S Lans 17 J5
Crawfordjohn
S Lans..................17 G5
Crawton Abers 49 L1
Creagan Inn
Ag & B.................43 J7
Creag Ghoraidh
W Isls..................85 c7
Creagorry W Isls......85 c7
Creaguaineach
Lodge Highld 44 E3
Creca D & G 9 M7
Creebank D & G 7 H6
Creebridge D & G 3 J2
Creetown D & G 3 K3
Creich Fife 38 E3
Cretshengan
Ag & B.................24 C5
Crianlarich Stirlg.....35 L3
Crichton Mdloth......29 K6
Crieff P & K.............37 H3
Crimond Abers.........69 K3
Crinaglack Highld.....64 C6
Crinan Ag & B..........34 A8
Crindledyke
N Lans..................27 L6
Croachy Highld........65 G8
Crocketford D & G ...8 E7
Croftamie Stirlg........26 E2
Croftown Highld.......72 F5
Crofts Moray 67 G4
Crofts of Dipple
Moray...................67 H3
Crofts of Savoch
Abers...................69 K3
Croggan Ag & B.......33 L3
Croick Highld...........74 B3
Cromarty Highld......75 H7
Crombie Fife 28 E2
Cromdale Highld 66 D8
Cromor W Isls..........84 f3
Cronberry E Ayrs......16 C5
Crookedholm
E Ayrs..................15 L3
Crook Inn Border.....17 L4
Crook of Devon
P & K...................37 L7
Cros W Isls..............84 g1
Crosbost W Isls........84 f3

Crossaig Ag & B 24 E7
Crossapol Ag & B......40 C7
Crossford Fife...........28 E2
Crossford S Lans......27 L8
Crossgatehall
E Loth...................29 K5
Crossgates E Ayrs.....15 J1
Crossgates Fife 28 F1
Crosshands E Ayrs....15 L4
Crosshill Fife 38 C7
Crosshill S Ayrs........15 J7
Crosshouse E Ayrs....15 K2
Cross Keys Ag & B....26 C2
Crosskirk Highld 82 F2
Crosslee Rens 26 D5
Crossmichael
D & G 4 C2
Cross of Jackston
Abers...................68 E7
Crossroads Abers....58 B4
Crossroads Abers....58 E6
Crosston Angus 48 E5
Crovie Abers.............68 F7
Crowhill E Loth 30 F4
Croy Highld..............65 J4
Croy N Lans 27 J3
Crubenmore
Highld..................55 G7
Cruden Bay Abers 69 K6
Cuaig Highld............61 L3
Cuan Ag & B 33 L4
Cuil Highld 43 J5
Culbokie Highld........64 F3
Culburnie Highld 64 D6
Culcabock Highld 65 G5
Culcharry Highld 65 K4
Culdrain Abers..........67 L7
Culduie Highld 61 L6
Culkein Highld..........76 C2
Culkein Drumbeg
Highld..................76 D2
Cullen Moray 67 L2
Cullerlie Abers..........58 E5
Cullicudden Highld...65 G2
Cuillin Hills Highld...51 G2
Cullipool Ag & B.......33 L5
Cullivoe Shet...........87 d2
Culloden Highld........65 H5
Culnacraig Highld.....76 C7
Culnaightrie D & G ...4 D5
Culnaknock
Highld..................61 H2
Culrain Highld 74 D3
Culross Fife 28 D2
Culroy S Ayrs...........15 H6
Culsalmond Abers....68 C7
Culscadden D & G....3 K5
Culshabbin D & G 3 G5
Culswick Shet...........87 b6
Cultercullen Abers ...59 H1
Cults C Aber.............59 G5
Culzean Castle &
Country Park
S Ayrs..................15 G7
Cumbernauld
N Lans..................27 K4
Cumbernauld
Village N Lans 27 K3
Cuminestown
Abers...................68 F4
Cumledge Border.....31 G6
Cummertrees
D & G 5 K2
Cummingston
Moray...................66 E1
Cumnock E Ayrs.......16 B5

Cumrue D & G 9 J5
Cunninghamhead
N Ayrs..................15 J2
Cunningsburgh
Shet....................87 c7
Cupar Fife................38 F4
Cupar Muir Fife 38 F5
Currie C Edin 29 G5
Cushnie Abers..........57 L3
Cutcloy D & G 3 J7
Cuthill Highld 75 G4

D

Dailly S Ayrs..............6 F2
Dairsie Fife...............39 G4
Dalabrog W Isls........85 b8
Dalavich Ag & B........34 D5
Dalbeattie D & G......4 E3
Dalcapon P & K.........46 F5
Dalchalm Highld 78 F7
Dalchreichart
Highld..................53 L3
Dalchruin P & K.........36 F4
Dalcrue P & K............37 L2
Daldowie
Crematorium
C Glas..................27 J6
Dalelia Highld...........42 E3
Dalgarven N Ayrs......15 H1
Dalgety Bay Fife 29 G2
Dalgig E Ayrs............16 B6
Dalginross P & K.......37 G3
Dalguise P & K..........46 F6
Dalhalvaig Highld......82 C5
Daliburgh W Isls........85 b8
Dalkeith Mdloth........29 K5
Dallas Moray.............66 D4
Dalmally Ag & B........35 H3
Dalmary Stirlg...........36 C7
Dalmellington
E Ayrs...................7 K2
Dalmeny C Edin........28 F3
Dalmore Highld 74 F7
Dalmuir W Duns.......26 E4
Dalnabreck Highld ...42 E3
Dalnacardoch
P & K...................46 B3
Dalnahaitnach
Highld..................55 K2
Dalnaspidal P & K.....45 K2
Dalnawillan
Lodge Highld.......82 F7
Daloist P & K............46 C5
Dalqueich P & K.......38 A6
Dalquhairn S Ayrs......7 G3
Dalreavoch Lodge
Highld..................78 D6
Dalry N Ayrs.............26 B7
Dalrymple E Ayrs......15 J6
Dalserf S Lans..........27 L7
Dalsmeran Ag & B....13 G6
Dalswinton D & G.....9 G5
Dalton D & G............9 K7
Dalveich Stirlg..........36 D3
Dalwhinnie Highld 54 F7
Damnaglaur
D & G 2 D7
Dandaleith Moray.....67 G5
Danderhall Mdloth....29 J4
Danshillock Abers.....68 D3
Danskine E Loth.......30 C5
Darnick Border.........19 H3
Darra Abers..............68 E5
Darvel E Ayrs............16 B2

Daugh of
Kinermony
Moray...................66 F6
Dava Highld..............66 C6
Davidson's Mains
C Edin..................29 G4
Davington D & G 9 M2
Daviot Abers.............68 E8
Daviot Highld............65 H6
Daviot House
Highld..................65 H6
Davoch of Grange
Moray...................67 K4
Deanburnhaugh
Border..................18 F6
Deans W Loth 28 D5
Deanshaugh
Moray...................67 H4
Deanston Stirlg.........36 F6
Dechmont W Loth....28 E4
Dechmont Road
W Loth..................28 D4
Degnish Ag & B........34 A5
Delfrigs Abers...........59 H2
Delliefure Highld.......66 D7
Delnabo Moray.........56 E3
Delnashaugh Inn
Moray...................66 E7
Delny Highld.............75 G6
Denbrae Fife.............38 F4
Denfield P & K..........37 K4
Denhead Abers.........69 J4
Denhead Fife............39 G5
Denhead of Gray
C Dund.................38 F2
Denholm Border.......19 J5
Denmore C Aber.......59 H3
Denny Falk...............27 L2
Dennyloanhead
Falk......................27 L3
Den of Lindores
Fife......................38 D4
Denside Abers..........58 F6
Derculich P & K........46 D5
Dervaig Ag & B.........41 K6
Deskford Moray........67 L3
Devonside Clacks 37 J7
Dewarton Mdloth 29 K5
Digg Highld..............70 C7
Dingwall Highld 64 E3
Dinnet Abers............57 K5
Dinwoodie D & G 9 K4
Dippen Ag & B..........13 K2
Dippen N Ayrs..........14 D5
Dipple Moray............67 H3
Dipple S Ayrs............6 E2
Dirleton E Loth 30 B2
Dochgarroch
Highld..................64 F6
Dodside E Rens........26 F7
Doll Highld...............78 F7
Dollar Clacks............37 K7
Dollarfield Clacks.....37 K7
Dolphinton S Lans ...28 F8
Donibristle Fife........29 G2
Doonfoot S Ayrs.......15 H5
Dorback Lodge
Highld..................56 D3
Dores Highld............64 F7
Dornie Highld...........52 D1
Dornoch Highld 75 H4
Dornock D & G 5 M2
Dorrery Highld..........82 F5
Douglas S Lans 17 G4
Douglas and
Angus C Dund.......39 G2

Douglas Pier
Ag & B 35 H7
Douglastown
Angus 48 C6
Douglas Water
S Lans 17 G3
Douglas West
S Lans 16 F3
Dounby Ork 86 b5
Doune Highld 73 L2
Doune Stirlg 36 F6
Dounepark S Ayrs 6 E3
Dounie Highld 74 D4
Dowally P & K 46 F6
Downfield C Dund 38 F2
Downhill P & K 38 A2
Downies Abers 59 H6
Draffan S Lans 16 F1
Drakemyre N Ayrs 26 B7
Dreghorn N Ayrs 15 J2
Drem E Loth 30 B3
Drimnin Highld 42 B5
Drimsallie Highld 43 J1
Dron P & K 38 B4
Drongan E Ayrs 15 K5
Dronley Angus 38 E1
Druimarbin Highld 43 L3
Druimavuic Ag & B .. 43 K7
Druimdrishaig
Ag & B 24 C4
Druimindarroch
Highld 51 L7
Drum Ag & B 24 F3
Drum P & K 37 L7
Drumalbin S Lans 17 H2
Drumbeg Highld 76 D3
Drumblade Abers 68 B6
Drumbreddon
D & G 2 C6
Drumbuie Highld 62 B7
Drumburn D & G 4 F4
Drumchapel C Glas .. 26 F4
Drumchastle P & K 45 L5
Drumclog S Lans 16 C2
Drumeldrie Fife 39 G6
Drumelzier Border 17 M3
Drumfearn Highld 51 L3
Drumfrennie
Abers 58 D5
Drumgley Angus 48 C6
Drumguish Highld 55 J5
Drumin Moray 66 E7
Drumjohn D & G 7 L3
Drumlamford
S Ayrs 7 G6
Drumlasie Abers 58 C4
Drumlemble
Ag & B 13 H5
Drumlithie Abers 49 J1
Drummoddie
D & G 3 H6
Drummore D & G 2 D7
Drummuir Moray 67 J5
Drumnadrochit
Highld 64 D7
Drumnagorrach
Moray 67 L4
Drumpark D & G 8 F6
Drumrunie Lodge
Highld 76 E7
Drumshang S Ayrs 15 G6
Drumuie Highld 61 G5
Drumuillie Highld 56 B2
Drumvaich Stirlg 36 E6
Drunzie P & K 38 B5
Drybridge Moray 67 K2

Drybridge N Ayrs 15 J3
Dryburgh Border 19 J3
Drymen Stirlg 26 E2
Drymuir Abers 69 G5
Drynoch Highld 60 F7
Dubford Abers 68 F2
Duchally Highld 77 J5
Duddingston
C Edin 29 J4
Dufftown Moray 67 H6
Duffus Moray 66 E2
Duirinish Highld 62 B7
Duisdalemore
Highld 51 L3
Duisky Highld 43 K2
Dull P & K 46 C6
Dullatur N Lans 27 K3
Dulnain Bridge
Highld 56 B1
Dumbarton
W Duns 26 D4
Dumfries D & G 9 G6
Dumgoyne Stirlg 26 F2
Dun Angus 49 G4
Dunalastair P & K 45 L5
Dunan Ag & B 25 K4
Dunan Highld 61 J8
Dunan P & K 45 G5
Dunaverty Ag & B 13 H7
Dunbar E Loth 30 E3
Dunbeath Highld 79 L3
Dunbeg Ag & B 34 C2
Dunblane Stirlg 37 G6
Dunbog Fife 38 E4
Duncanston
Highld 64 F3
Duncanstone
Abers 68 B8
Duncow D & G 9 G5
Duncrievie P & K 38 B5
Dundee C Dund 38 F2
Dundee Airport
C Dund 38 F2
Dundee
Crematorium
C Dund 38 F2
Dundonald S Ayrs 15 J3
Dundonnell Highld ... 72 E4
Dundreggan
Highld 53 L3
Dundrennan D & G 4 D5
Dunecht Abers 58 E4
Dunfermline Fife 28 F2
Dunfermline
Crematorium
Fife 28 F2
Dungavel S Lans 16 D3
Dunino Fife 39 J5
Dunipace Falk 27 L2
Dunkeld P & K 47 G7
Dunlappie Angus 48 F3
Dunlop E Ayrs 26 D8
Dunmaglass
Highld 54 F2
Dunmore Falk 28 B1
Dunnet Highld 83 J2
Dunnichen Angus 48 E6
Dunning P & K 37 L4
Dunoon Ag & B 25 K3
Dunphail Moray 66 C5
Dunragit D & G 2 E4
Duns Border 31 G2
Dunscore D & G 8 F5
Dunshalt Fife 38 D5
Dunshillock Abers 69 J5
Dunsyre S Lans 28 E8

Duntocher W Duns .. 26 E4
Duntulm Highld 70 C6
Dunure S Ayrs 15 G6
Dunvegan Highld 60 D5
Durisdeer D & G 8 F2
Durisdeermill
D & G 8 F2
Durness Highld 80 F3
Durno Abers 68 D8
Duror Highld 43 K5
Durran Ag & B 34 D5
Durris Abers 58 E6
Duthil Highld 55 L1
Dyce C Aber 59 G3
Dyke Moray 66 B3
Dykehead Angus 47 K5
Dykehead Angus 48 C4
Dykehead N Lans 28 B6
Dykehead Stirlg 36 D7
Dykelands Abers 49 H3
Dykends Angus 47 K5
Dykeside Abers 68 D5
Dysart Fife 38 E8

E

Eaglesfield D & G 9 M7
Eaglesham E Rens 27 G7
Earlish Highld 60 F3
Earlsferry Fife 39 H7
Earlsford Abers 68 F7
Earlston Border 19 J2
Earlston E Ayrs 15 K3
Easdale Ag & B 33 L4
Eassie and Nevay
Angus 48 B7
East Barns E Loth 30 F3
East Calder W Loth ... 28 E5
Easter Balmoral
Abers 57 G6
Easter Dalziel
Highld 65 H4
Easterhouse C Glas .. 27 J5
Easter Howgate
Mdloth 29 H5
Easter Kinkell
Highld 64 E4
Easter Moniack
Highld 64 E5
Easter Ord Abers 58 F4
Easter Pitkierie
Fife 39 J6
Easter Skeld Shet 87 c6
Easter Softlaw
Border 20 A3
Eastfield N Lans 28 B5
East Fortune
E Loth 30 C3
East Haven Angus 39 J1
East Helmsdale
Highld 79 H5
East Kilbride
S Lans 27 H7
Eastlands D & G 8 E7
East Linton E Loth 30 D3
East Morton D & G 8 F3
Eastriggs D & G 5 M2
East Saltoun
E Loth 30 B5
East Wemyss Fife 38 E7
East Whitburn
W Loth 28 C5
Ecclaw Border 30 F5
Ecclefechan D & G 9 L7
Eccles Border 20 A2

Ecclesmachan
W Loth 28 E4
Echt Abers 58 E4
Eckford Border 19 L4
Eday Ork 86 d4
Eday Airport Ork 86 d4
Edderton Highld 74 F4
Eddleston Border 29 H8
Eddlewood S Lans 27 J7
Edentaggart
Ag & B 35 K8
Edinbane Highld 60 E4
Edinburgh C Edin 29 H4
Edinburgh Airport
C Edin 28 F4
Edinburgh Castle
C Edin 29 H4
Edinburgh Old
& New Town
C Edin 29 H4
Edinburgh Royal
Botanic
Gardens C Edin 29 H4
Edinburgh Zoo
C Edin 29 G4
Edingham D & G 4 E3
Edington Border 31 J7
Ednam Border 19 L2
Edradynate P & K 46 D6
Edrom Border 31 H7
Edzell Angus 48 F3
Edzell Woods
Abers 49 G3
Effgill D & G 10 B4
Eigg Highld 51 G7
Eilanreach Highld 52 C2
Eilean Donan
Castle 52 D1
Elderslie Rens 26 E5
Elfhill Abers 58 F7
Elgin Moray 66 F4
Elgol Highld 51 H3
Elie Fife 39 H7
Ella Abers 68 C3
Ellary Ag & B 24 C3
Ellemford Border 30 F6
Ellenabeich Ag & B .. 33 L4
Elleric Ag & B 43 K6
Ellishader Highld 61 H2
Ellon Abers 69 H7
Elphin Highld 76 F6
Elphinstone E Loth ... 29 K4
Elrick Abers 58 F4
Elrig D & G 3 G5
Elsrickle S Lans 17 K2
Elvanfoot S Lans 17 J6
Elvingston E Loth 30 A4
Embo Highld 75 H3
Embo Street
Highld 75 H3
Enochdhu P & K 47 G4
Ensay Ag & B 41 J6
Enterkinfoot
D & G 8 E2
Eolaigearraidh
W Isls 85 b9
Erines Ag & B 24 E4
Eriska Ag & B 43 H7
Eriskay W Isls 85 c9
Errogie Highld 54 E2
Errol P & K 38 D3
Erskine Rens 26 E4
Ervie D & G 2 B2
Eskadale Highld 64 C6
Eskbank Mdloth 29 J5
Eskdalemuir D & G ... 10 A3

Essich Highld............65 G6
Esslemont Abers 69 H7
Etteridge Highld........55 G6
Ettrick Border 18 D6
Ettrickbridge
　Border...................18 F4
Ettrickhill Border......18 C6
Evanton Highld..........64 F2
Evelix Highld 75 G4
Evertown D & G........10 C6
Eyemouth Border 31 K5
Eyre Highld................60 F4

F

Faifley W Duns..........26 F4
Failford S Ayrs..........15 L4
Fairgirth D & G...........4 F7
Fair Isle Shet 87 e7
Fairlie N Ayrs............25 L7
Fairnilee Border 19 G3
Fala Mdloth 29 L6
Fala Dam Mdloth......29 L6
Falkirk Falk................28 B3
Falkirk
　Crematorium
　Falk......................28 B3
Falkirk Wheel Falk .. 28 A3
Falkland Fife...............38 D6
Fallburn S Lans 17 J2
Fallin Stirlg 37 H8
Falls of Blarghour
　Ag & B....................34 E5
Falnash Border..........10 D2
Fanagmore Highld....80 B5
Fanellan Highld 64 D5
Fanmore Ag & B........41 K7
Fannich Lodge
　Highld....................63 K2
Fans Highld 19 J2
Farmtown Moray........67 L4
Farnell Angus............49 G5
Farr Highld 55 K5
Farr Highld 65 G7
Farr Highld 81 L3
Farraline Highld.........54 E2
Fasnacloich
　Ag & B....................43 K6
Fasnakyle Highld.......63 L8
Fassfern Highld 43 K2
Fauldhouse
　W Loth...................28 C6
Fearn Highld 75 H6
Fearnan P & K...........46 B7
Fearnbeg Highld........62 B3
Fearnmore Highld......61 L3
Fearnoch Ag & B.......24 F3
Fenton Barns
　E Loth....................30 B3
Fenwick E Ayrs 15 L2
Feolin Ferry
　Ag & B....................23 H4
Fergushill N Ayrs 15 J2
Feriniquarrie
　Highld....................60 B4
Fern Angus................48 D4
Ferness Highld..........66 B5
Fernie Fife..................38 E4
Ferniegair S Lans......27 K7
Fernilea Highld...........60 F7
Ferrindonald
　Highld....................51 K4
Ferryden Angus 49 H5
Ferry Point Highld 75 G4
Ferrytown Highld 75 G4

Fersit Highld..............44 F2
Feshiebridge
　Highld....................55 K4
Fetlar Shet 87 e2
Fetterangus Abers....69 J4
Fettercairn Abers......49 G2
Fiag Lodge Highld 77 K3
Fife Keith Moray........67 J4
Finavon Angus 48 D5
Fincharn Ag & B.........34 C6
Findhorn Moray..........66 C2
Findhorn Bridge
　Highld....................65 J8
Findochty Moray........67 K2
Findo Gask P & K......37 L4
Findon Abers 59 H6
Findon Mains
　Highld....................64 F3
Findrack House
　Abers.....................58 B4
Fingask P & K...........38 C4
Fingland D & G..........16 E6
Finlarig Stirlg 36 C1
Finnart P & K.............45 H5
Finsbay W Isls 84 d5
Finstown Ork.............86 b6
Fintry Abers 68 E4
Fintry Stirlg 27 H2
Finzean Abers...........58 B6
Fionnphort Ag & B....32 D3
Fionnsbhagh
　W Isls 84 d5
Fishcross Clacks.......37 J7
Fisherford Abers........68 C7
Fisherrow E Loth.......29 K4
Fisherton Highld 65 H4
Fisherton S Ayrs 15 H6
Fishnish Pier
　Ag & B....................42 D7
Fiskavaig Highld........60 E7
Fladdabister Shet 87 c6
Flashader Highld 60 E4
Flemington S Lans 27 H6
Flodigarry Highld 70 C6
Fochabers Moray........67 H3
Fogo Border 31 G8
Fogwatt Moray...........66 F3
Foindle Highld 80 B5
Folda Angus 47 J4
Folla Rule Abers 68 D7
Forbestown Abers.....57 H3
Ford Ag & B...............34 C6
Fordell Fife................29 G2
Fordoun Abers 49 J2
Fordyce Abers 68 B2
Forest Mill Clacks......37 K8
Forfar Angus..............48 D6
Forgandenny
　P & K.....................38 A4
Forgie Moray.............67 J4
Forgieside Moray 67 J4
Forgue Abers 68 B5
Fornighty Highld........65 L4
Forres Moray.............66 C3
Forse Highld 79 M2
Forsinard Highld 82 C6
Fort Augustus
　Highld....................54 B4
Forteviot P & K...........37 L4
Forth S Lans 28 C7
Fortingall P & K..........46 B6
Fortrie Abers..............68 C5
Fortrose Highld 65 H3
Fort William
　Highld....................43 L2
Foss P & K.................46 C5

Foula Shet 87 a6
Foulden Border 31 J7
Fountainhall
　Border...................29 L8
Fourpenny Highld......75 H3
Foveran Abers 59 H2
Fowlis Angus 38 E2
Fowlis Wester
　P & K.....................37 J3
Foxbar Rens..............26 E6
Foyers Highld............54 D2
Foynesfield Highld.....65 L4
Fraserburgh Abers ...69 J2
Frenich P & K.............46 C5
Freswick Highld.........83 L3
Freuchie Fife..............38 E6
Friockheim Angus......48 F6
Frogden Border 20 B4
Fuinary Highld 42 C6
Fullarton N Ayrs 15 H2
Fullwood E Ayrs.........26 E7
Funtullich P & K.........36 F3
Furnace Ag & B..........34 E7
Fyvie Abers 68 E6

G

Gabroc Hill E Ayrs 26 E7
Gadgirth S Ayrs.........15 K5
Gailes N Ayrs 15 H3
Gairloch Highld..........71 J6
Gairlochy Highld........53 J8
Gairneybridge
　P & K.....................38 B7
Galashiels Border 19 G3
Gallanachbeg
　Ag & B....................34 B2
Gallanachmore
　Ag & B....................34 B3
Gallatown Fife............38 E8
Gallovie Highld...........54 E7
Galloway Forest
　Park 7 J5
Gallowfauld Angus.....38 D7
Gallowhill P & K.........38 B1
Galltair Highld............52 C2
Galston E Ayrs 15 L3
Gamrie Abers.............68 F2
Ganavan Bay
　Ag & B....................34 B2
Gannachy Angus........48 F3
Garbity Moray............67 H4
Garbole Highld...........55 H1
Garchory Abers 57 G4
Gardenstown
　Abers.....................68 F2
Garderhouse
　Shet......................87 c5
Garelochhead
　Ag & B....................25 L1
Gargunnock Stirlg.....36 F8
Garlieston D & G.........3 K5
Garlogie Abers...........58 E4
Garmond Abers 68 F4
Garmouth Moray........67 H2
Garnkirk N Lans 27 J5
Garrabost W Isls 84 g2
Garralian E Ayrs 16 B5
Garroch D & G.............7 M6
Garrochty Ag & B......25 J7
Garros Highld.............61 H2
Gartachossan
　Ag & B....................23 G6
Gartcosh N Lans 27 J5

Garthamlock
　C Glas...................27 H5
Gartly Abers 67 L7
Gartmore Stirlg.........36 C7
Gartness N Lans 27 K5
Gartness Stirlg 26 F2
Gartocharn
　W Duns..................26 D2
Gartymore Highld 79 H5
Garvald E Loth..........30 D4
Garvan Highld............43 J2
Garvard Ag & B..........23 G1
Garve Highld 64 B3
Garvellachs Ag & B...33 K5
Garvock Inver 26 B4
Garyvard W Isls........84 f3
Gatehead E Ayrs.......15 K3
Gatehouse of
　Fleet D & G 3 M4
Gateshaw Border 20 B5
Gateside Angus 48 D7
Gateside E Rens 26 E6
Gateside Fife..............38 C5
Gateside N Ayrs 26 C7
Gateslack D & G 8 F2
Gattonside Border 19 H3
Gauldry Fife...............38 F3
Gauldswell P & K.......47 K6
Gavinton Border........31 G7
Gearraidh Bhaird
　W Isls 84 f3
Geary Highld 60 D3
Gellyburn P & K 47 H8
Gelston D & G 4 D3
Georgefield D & G 10 B4
Georgemas
　Junction
　Station Highld 83 H4
Georth Ork.................86 b5
Giffnock E Rens.........27 G6
Gifford E Loth 30 C5
Giffordtown Fife........38 E5
Gigha Ag & B..............23 L7
Gilchriston E Loth......30 B5
Gillen Highld...............60 D3
Gillesbie D & G 9 K4
Gillock Highld 83 J4
Gills Highld 83 K2
Gilmanscleuch
　Border...................18 E5
Gilmerton C Edin 29 J5
Gilmerton P & K........37 J3
Gilston Border 29 L6
Girdle Toll N Ayrs 15 J2
Girlsta Shet...............87 c5
Girthon D & G 4 A4
Girvan S Ayrs 6 E3
Gladsmuir E Loth......29 M4
Glamis Angus 48 C6
Glasgow C Glas 27 G5
Glasgow Airport
　Rens......................26 E5
Glasgow Science
　Centre C Glas 27 G5
Glasnacardoch
　Bay Highld.............51 L6
Glasnakille Highld......51 H3
Glassford S Lans 27 J8
Glasterlaw Angus......48 F6
Glebe Highld 54 D2
Gledpark D & G 4 B5
Glenallachie Moray ...67 G6
Glenancross
　Highld....................51 K6
Glenaros House
　Ag & B....................42 B7

Glenbarr Ag & B........13 H3
Glenbarry Abers.......68 B4
Glenbeg Highld.........42 C4
Glenbervie Abers......49 J1
Glenboig N Lans........27 J5
Glenborrodale
    Highld................42 C4
Glenbranter
    Ag & B...............35 G7
Glenbreck Border.....17 K5
Glenbrittle House
    Highld................50 F2
Glenbuck E Ayrs.......16 E4
Glencally Angus.......48 B4
Glencaple D & G........5 H2
Glencarron Lodge
    Highld................63 G4
Glencarse P & K.......38 C3
Glen Clunie Lodge
    Abers.................56 E8
Glencoe Highld.........43 L5
Glencothe Border.....17 L4
Glencraig Fife.........38 C7
Glencrosh D & G........8 D4
Glendale Highld........60 B4
Glendaruel Ag & B...25 G2
Glendevon P & K.......37 K6
Glendoe Lodge
    Highld................54 C4
Glendoick P & K.......38 C3
Glenduckie Fife.......38 D4
Glenegedale
    Ag & B...............22 F7
Glenelg Highld.........52 C2
Glenerney Moray......66 C5
Glenfarg P & K.........38 B5
Glenfinnan Highld....43 H1
Glenfintaig Lodge
    Highld................53 K7
Glenfoot P & K.........38 C4
Glenfyne Lodge
    Ag & B...............35 H4
Glengarnock
    N Ayrs................26 C7
Glengolly Highld......83 G3
Glengorm Castle
    Ag & B...............41 K5
Glengrasco Highld....61 G5
Glenholm Border......17 L3
Glenhoul D & G.........8 A5
Glenisla Angus........44 K4
Glenkin Ag & B.........25 K3
Glenkindie Abers.....57 K3
Glenlivet Moray.......66 F8
Glenlochar D & G.......4 C3
Glenlomond P & K....38 C6
Glenluce D & G.........2 E4
Glenmassen
    Ag & B...............25 J2
Glenmavis N Lans....27 K5
Glenmore Highld.....61 G6
Glenmore Lodge
    Highld................56 B4
Glen Nevis House
    Highld................44 B3
Glenochil Clacks......37 H7
Glenquiech Angus....48 C4
Glenralloch Ag & B...24 E5
Glenrothes Fife.......38 D7
Glenshero Lodge
    Highld................54 E6
Glenstriven Ag & B...25 J3
Glen Trool Lodge
    D & G..................7 J2
Glentrool Village
    D & G..................7 H6

Glentruim House
    Highld................55 G6
Glenuig Highld.........42 D2
Glenvarragill
    Highld................61 G6
Glenwhilly D & G........6 E7
Glespin S Lans.........16 F4
Glutt Lodge Highld...79 H2
Gogar C Edin............29 G4
Gollanfield Highld....65 J4
Golspie Highld..........75 H2
Gonfirth Shet..........87 c4
Goosecruives
    Abers.................58 E8
Gordon Border........19 K2
Gordon Arms
    Hotel Border......18 D4
Gordonstown
    Abers.................68 B3
Gordonstown
    Abers.................68 D6
Gorebridge Mdloth..29 K6
Gorrachie Abers......68 E3
Gorstan Highld........64 B2
Gorten Ag & B.........33 L2
Gorthleck Highld.....54 E2
Gourdas Abers.........68 E6
Gourdie C Dund........38 F2
Gourdon Abers.........49 K3
Gourock Inver.........25 L3
Govan C Glas............26 F5
Gower Highld...........64 D3
Gowkhall Fife..........28 E1
Grabhair W Isls........84 f3
Gramsdal W Isls......85 c6
Gramsade W Isls......85 c6
Grandtully P & K......46 E5
Grange P & K...........38 D3
Grange
    Crossroads
    Moray................67 K4
Grange Hall Moray...66 C3
Grangehall S Lans....17 J2
Grangemouth Falk...28 C3
Grange of
    Lindores Fife......38 D4
Grangepans Falk......28 D3
Granton C Edin.........29 H3
Grantown-on-
    Spey Highld........66 C8
Grantshouse
    Border................31 G5
Gravir W Isls...........84 f3
Great Cumbrae
    Island N Ayrs......25 K6
Greenburn W Loth...28 C6
Greenfield Ag & B....25 M1
Greenfield Highld....53 J5
Greengairs N Lans...27 K4
Greenhill D & G........9 J6
Greenhill Falk..........27 L3
Greenhill S Lans......17 H3
Greenholm E Ayrs...16 B3
Greenhouse
    Border................19 H5
Greenland Highld.....83 J3
Greenlaw Border......19 L1
Greenlea D & G.........9 H6
Greenloaning
    P & K..................37 H6
Greenock Inver........26 B3
Greenock
    Crematorium
    Inver.................26 B3
Greenshields
    S Lans................17 K2

Greosabhagh
    W Isls.................84 e4
Greshornish
    House Hotel
    Highld................60 E4
Gretna D & G...........10 B8
Gretna Green
    D & G..................10 B8
Gretna Services
    D & G..................10 B7
Greyrigg D & G..........9 J4
Greystone Angus.....48 E7
Grimmet S Ayrs.......15 H7
Grimshader W Isls...84 f3
Griomaisiader
    W Isls.................84 f3
Griomsaigh W Isls...85 c6
Grishipoll Ag & B.....40 F4
Gritley Ork...............86 d6
Grogarry W Isls........85 b7
Grogport Ag & B.......13 K1
Groigearraidh
    W Isls.................85 b7
Grosebay W Isls.......84 e4
Gruinard Highld.......71 L4
Gruinart Ag & B.......22 F5
Grula Highld............60 F8
Gruline Ag & B.........42 B7
Gruting Shet...........87 c5
Gualachulain
    Highld................44 B7
Guardbridge Fife....39 G4
Guay P & K...............46 F6
Guildtown P & K.......38 B2
Guiltreehill S Ayrs...15 J7
Gullane E Loth.........30 B2
Gunnista Shet.........87 d6
Gutcher Shet...........87 d2
Guthrie Angus.........48 F6

H

Hackland Ork...........86 c5
Hadden Border.........20 B3
Haddington E Loth...30 B4
Haddo Abers............68 F6
Haggersta Shet.......87 c5
Haggs Falk...............27 L3
Halbeath Fife..........28 F1
Halcro Highld...........83 J4
Halket E Ayrs...........26 D7
Halkirk Highld.........83 G4
Hall E Rens..............26 D7
Hall Glen Falk..........28 B3
Hallin Highld............60 D3
Hallyne Border........18 B2
Hamilton S Lans.......27 J7
Hamilton Services
    S Lans................27 J6
Hamnavoe Shet.......87 c6
Handa Island
    Highld................80 A6
Happendon
    S Lans................17 G3
Happendon
    Services S Lans...17 G3
Hardgate Abers.......58 E5
Hardgate D & G.........4 E2
Hardgate W Duns.....26 F4
Harelaw Border.......19 H5
Harelaw D & G.........10 B2
Harlosh Highld.........60 D6
Haroldswick Shet.....87 e1
Harpsdale Highld.....83 G4
Harrapool Highld.....51 K2

Harrietfield P & K.....37 K2
Harris W Isls............84 d4
Harthill N Lans........28 B5
Hartwood N Lans.....27 L6
Hartwoodmyres
    Border................18 F4
Haster Highld..........83 K5
Hatton Abers...........69 K6
Hatton Angus..........48 D7
Hatton of Fintray
    Abers.................58 F3
Haugh E Ayrs...........15 L4
Haughhead
    E Duns................27 G3
Haugh of Glass
    Moray................67 J6
Haugh of Urr
    D & G..................4 E2
Haughs of
    Kinnaird Angus...49 G5
Hawick Border.........19 G6
Hawksland S Lans....17 G2
Hayfield Ag & B........34 F3
Hayhillock Angus.....48 E7
Hazelbank S Lans....17 G1
Hazelton Walls
    Fife...................38 E3
Headlesscross
    N Lans................28 B6
Heart of Scotland
    Services N Lans...28 B5
Heast Highld...........51 K2
Heath Hall D & G.......9 H6
Heglibister Shet......87 c5
Heiton Border.........19 L4
Helensburgh
    Ag & B...............26 B2
Helenton S Ayrs.......15 K3
Helmsdale Highld....79 H5
Hempriggs Moray....66 D2
Heribusta Highld.....70 B7
Heriot Border..........29 L7
Hermiston C Edin.....29 G4
Hermitage Border....10 E3
Heronsford
    S Ayrs..................6 D5
Herston Ork.............86 c7
Hestwall Ork............86 b5
Heughhead Abers....57 J3
Heugh Head
    Border................31 H6
Heylipoll Ag & B.......40 C7
Heylor Shet.............87 c3
High Ardwell
    D & G..................2 C6
High Auldgirth
    D & G..................8 F5
High Blantyre
    S Lans................27 J6
High Bonnybridge
    Falk..................27 L3
High Cross E Ayrs....15 K1
High Drummore
    D & G..................2 D7
Highfield N Ayrs......26 C7
High Pennyvenie
    E Ayrs................15 L7
Hightae D & G..........9 J6
High Valleyfield
    Fife...................28 D2
Hillend Fife............28 F2
Hill End Fife............37 L7
Hillend Mdloth........29 H5
Hillend N Lans.........27 L5
Hillhead Abers.........68 B7
Hillhead S Lans........17 J2

Hillhead of
Cocklaw Abers 69 K5
Hilliclay Highld 83 H3
Hillington C Glas 26 F5
Hill of Beath Fife 28 F1
Hill of Fearn
Highld 75 H5
Hillowton D & G........ 4 D3
Hillside Abers 59 H5
Hillside Angus 49 H4
Hillswick Shet 87 c3
Hillwell Shet 87 C8
Hilton Border 31 H7
Hilton Highld 75 J6
Hirn Abers................. 58 D5
Hobkirk Border........ 19 J7
Hoddom Cross
D & G 9 L7
Hoddom Mains
D & G 9 K7
Hollandstoun Ork 86 e3
Hollee D & G 10 A7
Hollows D & G 10 C6
Hollybush E Ayrs.... 15 K6
Holmhead E Ayrs...... 16 B5
Holmsford Bridge
Crematorium
N Ayrs 15 J2
Holytown N Lans...... 27 K6
Holytown
Crematorium
N Lans 27 K6
Holywood D & G........ 9 G6
Holywood Village
D & G 9 G6
Hopehouse Border .. 18 D6
Hopeman Moray...... 66 E1
Horndean Border 31 J8
Horra Shet................. 87 d2
Horsleyhill Border.... 19 H5
Hoscote Border........ 18 F6
Hosh P & K............... 37 H3
Hoswick Shet............ 87 C7
Houndslow Border .. 30 D8
Houndwood
Border 31 H5
Househill Highld...... 65 L4
Housieside Abers 59 G1
Houston Rens 26 D5
Houstry Highld 79 K2
Houton Ork 86 b6
Howe Highld 83 K3
Howe of Teuchar
Abers..................... 68 E5
Howes D & G 5 L2
Howgate Mdloth...... 29 H6
Howmore W Isls...... 85 b7
Hownam Border........ 20 B5
Howwood Rens........ 26 D6
Hoy Ork 86 b7
Humbie E Loth.......... 30 B5
Hume Border 19 L2
Huna Highld 83 L2
Hundalee Border...... 19 K5
Hunter's Quay
Ag & B 25 K3
Hunthill Lodge
Angus..................... 48 D3
Huntington E Loth... 30 B4
Huntly Abers............. 67 L6
Hurlford E Ayrs........ 15 L3
Hurtiso Ork............... 86 c6
Hutton Border 31 J7
Hyndford Bridge
S Lans 17 H2
Hynish Ag & B........... 40 C8

I

Ichrachan Ag & B 34 E2
Idrigill Highld............ 60 F2
Imachar N Ayrs........ 13 L2
Inchbae Lodge
Hotel Highld........ 73 K7
Inchbare Angus........ 48 F4
Inchberry Moray....... 67 G4
Incheril Highld 63 G3
Inchinnan Rens 26 E5
Inchlaggan Highld.... 53 J5
Inchmichael P & K.... 38 D3
Inchnacardoch
Hotel Highld........ 54 B3
Inchnadamph
Highld 76 F4
Inchture P & K 38 D2
Inchvuilt Highld........ 63 K6
Inchyra P & K............ 38 C4
Ingleston D & G 5 G2
Inkhorn Abers........... 69 H6
Inkstack Highld......... 83 J2
Innellan Ag & B 25 K4
Innerleithen
Border 18 E3
Innerleven Fife........ 38 F7
Innermessan
D & G 2 C3
Innerwick E Loth...... 30 F4
Innesmill Moray....... 67 G2
Insch Abers............... 68 C8
Insh Highld 55 J5
Inver Abers............... 56 F6
Inver Highld 75 J5
Inver P & K............... 46 F7
Inverailort Highld..... 42 F1
Inveralligin Highld.... 62 C3
Inverallochy Abers.... 69 K2
Inveran Highld 74 D2
Inveraray Ag & B....... 34 F5
Inverarish Highld...... 61 J7
Inverarity Angus...... 48 D7
Inverarnan Stirlg..... 35 K4
Inverasdale Highld... 71 K4
Inverbeg Ag & B 35 K7
Inverbervie Abers.... 49 K2
Inver-boyndie
Abers..................... 68 C2
Invercreran
House Hotel
Ag & B 43 K6
Inverdruie Highld..... 55 L3
Inveresk E Loth........ 29 K4
Inveresragan
Ag & B 34 E1
Inverey Abers 56 D7
Inverfarigaig
Highld 54 D2
Inverfolla Ag & B 43 J7
Invergarry Highld..... 53 L5
Invergeldie P & K..... 36 F2
Invergloy Highld....... 53 K7
Invergordon
Highld 74 F7
Invergowrie P & K.... 38 F2
Inverguseran
Highld 52 B4
Inverhadden P & K.... 45 L5
Inverherive Hotel
Stirlg 35 L3
Inverie Highld 52 B5
Inverinan Ag & B 34 E4
Inverinate Highld..... 52 E2
Inverkeilor Angus.... 49 G6

Inverkeithing Fife.... 28 F2
Inverkeithny
Abers..................... 68 C5
Inverkip Inver 25 L4
Inverkirkaig
Highld 76 C4
Inverlael Highld 72 F4
Inverlair Highld......... 44 E1
Inverliever Lodge
Ag & B 34 C6
Inverlochy Ag & B 35 H2
Invermark Angus..... 48 D1
Invermoriston
Highld 54 C3
Invernaver Highld..... 81 L4
Inverness Highld 65 G5
Inverness Airport
Highld 65 J4
Inverness
Crematorium
Highld 64 F5
Invernoaden
Ag & B 35 G7
Inveroran Hotel
Ag & B 44 D7
Inverquharity
Angus..................... 48 C5
Inverquhomery
Abers..................... 69 J5
Inverroy Highld 53 K8
Inversanda Highld.... 43 J4
Invershiel Highld...... 52 E2
Invershin Highld 74 D3
Invershore Highld..... 83 J8
Inversnaid Hotel
Stirlg 35 K5
Inverugie Abers........ 69 L5
Inveruglas Ag & B 35 K5
Inveruglass Highld... 55 J5
Inverurie Abers........ 58 E2
Iochdar W Isls.......... 85 b7
Iona Ag & B............... 32 D3
Ironmacannie
D & G 8 B6
Irvine N Ayrs............ 15 H2
Isauld Highld 82 E3
Isbister Shet............ 87 c2
Isbister Shet............ 87 d4
Islay Ag & B 23 G4
Islay Airport Ag & B.. 22 F7
Isle of Lewis W Isls .. 84 f2
Isle of Mull Ag & B... 33 J1
Isle of Skye Highld ... 60 F6
Isle of Whithorn
D & G 3 K7
Isleornsay Highld..... 51 L3
Islesteps D & G......... 9 G7
Islibhig W Isls........... 84 d3
Islivig W Isls............. 84 d3

J

Jackton S Lans.......... 27 G7
Jamestown Highld.... 64 D3
Jamestown
W Duns................. 26 D3
Janetstown Highld.... 79 L3
Janetstown Highld.... 83 L5
Jardine Hall D & G 9 J5
Jawcraig Falk........... 27 L4
Jedburgh Border...... 19 K5
Jemimaville Highld .. 65 H2
John o' Groats
Highld 83 L2
Johnshaven Abers.... 49 J3

Johnstone D & G 9 M3
Johnstone Rens 26 D5
Johnstonebridge
D & G 9 J4
Joppa C Edin 29 J4
Joppa S Ayrs 15 K5
Juniper Green
C Edin 29 G5
Jura Ag & B 23 J2

K

Kaimend S Lans 17 J1
Kames Ag & B 25 G4
Kames E Ayrs............ 16 D4
Keig Abers 58 B2
Keilarsbrae Clacks 37 J8
Keillour P & K............ 37 K3
Keiloch Abers............ 56 E6
Keils Ag & B 23 K5
Keir Mill D & G 8 E4
Keiss Highld.............. 83 L4
Keith Moray.............. 67 J4
Keithick P & K 47 K8
Keithock Angus........ 48 F4
Keithtown Highld...... 64 E3
Kelhead D & G 5 K2
Kellas Angus............. 39 G1
Kellas Moray............. 66 E4
Kelloholm D & G........ 16 E4
Kelso Border 19 L3
Keltneyburn P & K.... 46 B6
Kelton D & G 9 H7
Kelty Fife 38 B8
Kemback Fife 39 G4
Kemnay Abers 58 E3
Kenmore Highld 62 B3
Kenmore P & K 46 B7
Kennacraig Ag & B.... 24 D5
Kennet Clacks 28 C1
Kennethmont
Abers..................... 67 L8
Kennoway Fife.......... 38 F6
Kenovay Ag & B........ 40 C6
Kensaleyre Highld.... 60 F4
Kentallen Highld....... 43 K5
Kentra Highld............ 42 D3
Keoldale Highld 80 F3
Keppoch Highld......... 52 D1
Kerrera Ag & B.......... 34 B2
Kerrycroy Ag & B 25 J6
Kershader W Isls....... 84 f3
Kettins P & K 47 K8
Kettlebridge Fife 38 E6
Kettleholm D & G 9 K6
Kettletoft Ork........... 86 d4
Kidsdale D & G........... 3 J7
Kiel Crofts Ag & B..... 43 H8
Kiells Ag & B 23 H5
Kilbarchan Rens 26 D5
Kilbeg Highld............ 51 K4
Kilberry Ag & B 24 C5
Kilbirnie N Ayrs 26 C7
Kilbride Ag & B.......... 24 C3
Kilbride Ag & B.......... 25 H5
Kilbuiack Moray........ 66 D3
Kilchamaig Ag & B.... 24 D6
Kilchattan Ag & B..... 25 J7
Kilchattan Ag & B..... 32 E7
Kilcheran Ag & B 43 G8
Kilchoan Highld 41 L4
Kilchoman Ag & B..... 22 D5
Kilchrenan Ag & B.... 34 E3
Kilconquhar Fife 39 H6
Kilcoy Highld............ 64 E4

Kilcreggan Ag & B....25 L3
Kildalloig Ag & B......13 J5
Kildary Highld 75 G6
Kildavaig Ag & B......25 G5
Kildavanan Ag & B....25 H5
Kildonan Highld.......79 G4
Kildonan N Ayrs........14 D5
Kildonan Lodge
    Highld..................78 F4
Kildonnan Highld 51 G7
Kildrochet House
    D & G.....................2 C4
Kildrummy Abers......57 K2
Kilfinan Ag & B..........24 F3
Kilfinnan Highld........53 K6
Kilgrammie S Ayrs......6 F2
Kilkenneth Ag & B.....40 B7
Kilkenzie Ag & B.......13 H4
Kilkerran Ag & B.......13 J5
Killearn Stirlg 26 F2
Killen Highld..............65 G3
Killichonan P & K......45 J5
Killiechonate
    Highld..................44 D1
Killiechronan
    Ag & B..................42 B7
Killiecrankie P & K.....46 E4
Killilan Highld............62 E7
Killimster Highld........83 K4
Killin Stirlg 36 C2
Killochyett
    Border..................19 G1
Kilmacolm Inver 26 C4
Kilmahog Stirlg.........36 D5
Kilmahumaig
    Ag & B..................34 A8
Kilmaluag Highld......70 C6
Kilmany Fife..............38 F3
Kilmarnock E Ayrs.....15 K2
Kilmartin Ag & B.......34 B7
Kilmaurs E Ayrs........15 K2
Kilmelford Ag & B 34 B5
Kilmichael Ag & B.....13 H5
Kilmichael
    Glassary Ag & B....34 B8
Kilmichael of
    Inverlussa
    Ag & B..................24 D2
Kilmorack Highld......64 D5
Kilmore Ag & B.........34 C3
Kilmore Highld..........51 K4
Kilmory Ag & B.........24 C4
Kilmory Highld..........42 B3
Kilmory N Ayrs..........14 B5
Kilmuir Highld..........60 D5
Kilmuir Highld..........65 G4
Kilmuir Highld..........70 B7
Kilmuir Highld..........75 G6
Kilmun Ag & B..........25 K3
Kilnave Ag & B.........22 F4
Kilncadzow S Lans ...28 B8
Kilninver Ag & B.......34 B3
Kiloran Ag & B..........32 E7
Kilpatrick N Ayrs.......14 A4
Kilrenny Fife..............39 J6
Kilspindie P & K........38 C3
Kilstay D & G 2 D7
Kilsyth N Lans 27 J3
Kiltarlity Highld 64 D6
Kilvaxter Highld........70 B7
Kilwinning N Ayrs......15 H2
Kinbrace Highld........78 F3
Kinbuck Stirlg 37 G6
Kincaple Fife.............39 G4
Kincardine Fife.........28 C2
Kincardine Highld 74 E4

Kincardine O'Neil
    Abers....................58 B5
Kinclaven P & K........47 J8
Kincorth C Aber........59 H5
Kincorth House
    Moray...................66 C3
Kincraig Highld.........55 K4
Kincraigie P & K........46 F6
Kindallachan P & K...46 F6
Kinerarach Ag & B....24 B7
Kinfauns P & K.........38 C3
Kingarth Ag & B.......25 J6
Kingcausie Abers 59 G5
Kingholm Quay
    D & G.....................9 G7
Kinghorn Fife............29 H2
Kinglassie Fife..........38 D7
Kingoldrum
    Angus...................48 B5
Kingoodie P & K........38 E2
Kingsbarns Fife.........39 K5
Kingsburgh Highld....60 F4
Kingscross N Ayrs.....14 D4
Kingseat Fife............28 F1
Kingsford C Aber......58 F4
Kingsford E Ayrs.......26 E8
Kings House Hotel
    Highld..................44 D5
Kingshouse Hotel
    Stirlg....................36 C4
Kingskettle Fife........38 E5
Kingsmuir Angus......48 D6
Kings Muir Border 18 C2
Kingsmuir Fife..........39 J5
Kingston E Loth........30 C3
Kingston on Spey
    Moray...................67 H2
Kingswells C Aber 59 G4
Kingussie Highld.......55 H5
Kinharrachie
    Abers....................69 H7
Kinharvie D & G 5 G2
Kinkell Bridge
    P & K....................37 J4
Kinknockie Abers......69 J6
Kinleith C Edin 29 G5
Kinloch Highld 50 F5
Kinloch Highld 77 H2
Kinloch Highld 81 H5
Kinloch P & K 47 J7
Kinlochard Stirlg 36 B6
Kinlochbervie
    Highld..................80 C4
Kinlocheil Highld 43 J1
Kinlochewe Highld....62 F3
Kinloch Hourn
    Highld..................52 E4
Kinlochlaggan
    Highld..................54 E7
Kinlochleven
    Highld..................44 C4
Kinlochmoidart
    Highld..................42 E2
Kinlochnanuagh
    Highld..................52 B8
Kinloch Rannoch
    P & K....................45 L5
Kinloss Moray...........66 C3
Kinmuck Abers..........58 F2
Kinmundy Abers 59 G2
Kinnabus Ag & B.......12 B2
Kinnadie Abers..........69 H5
Kinnaird P & K..........46 F5
Kinneff Abers............49 K2
Kinnelhead D & G......9 H2
Kinnell Angus............48 F6

Kinnesswood
    P & K....................38 C6
Kinnordy Angus 48 B5
Kinross P & K............38 B6
Kinrossie P & K.........38 C2
Kinross Services
    P & K....................38 B6
Kintail Highld 52 F2
Kintessack Moray......66 B3
Kintillo P & K............38 B4
Kintore Abers............58 E3
Kintour Ag & B..........23 H7
Kintra Ag & B 22 F8
Kintra Ag & B 32 D3
Kintraw Ag & B.........34 B6
Kintyre Ag & B 13 J2
Kinveachy Highld......55 L2
Kippen Stirlg 36 E7
Kippford or Scaur
    D & G.....................4 E4
Kirbister Ork 86 b6
Kirk Highld................83 K4
Kirkabister Shet 87 d6
Kirkandrews D & G 4 A5
Kirkbean D & G 5 G3
Kirkbuddo Angus......48 E7
Kirkburn Border 18 D2
Kirkcaldy Fife...........38 D8
Kirkcaldy
    Crematorium
    Fife......................38 D8
Kirkchrist D & G........4 B5
Kirkcolm D & G 2 B2
Kirkconnel D & G......16 E6
Kirkconnell D & G 5 G2
Kirkcowan D & G 3 G3
Kirkcudbright
    D & G.....................4 B5
Kirkfieldbank
    S Lans 17 G2
Kirkgunzeon
    D & G.....................4 F2
Kirkhill Highld 64 E5
Kirkhope S Lans 17 J7
Kirkibost Highld........51 H2
Kirkinch P & K...........47 L7
Kirkinner D & G 3 J5
Kirkintilloch
    E Duns..................27 H4
Kirkland D & G 8 E4
Kirkland D & G 9 H4
Kirkland D & G 16 E6
Kirkliston C Edin.......28 F4
Kirkmabreck D & G 3 K4
Kirkmaiden D & G......2 D7
Kirkmichael P & K 47 H4
Kirkmichael
    S Ayrs...................15 J7
Kirkmuirhill S Lans ...16 F2
Kirknewton
    W Loth..................28 F5
Kirkney Abers............67 L7
Kirk of Shotts
    N Lans..................21 L5
Kirkoswald S Ayrs.....15 G2
Kirkpatrick D & G 8 F4
Kirkpatrick
    Durham D & G 8 D7
Kirkpatrick-
    Fleming D & G........10 B7
Kirkstile Abers 67 L7
Kirkstile D & G 10 C4
Kirkstyle Highld........83 L2
Kirkton Abers............58 C1
Kirkton D & G.............9 G6
Kirkton Fife...............38 F3

Kirkton Highld 62 C8
Kirkton Highld 62 D6
Kirkton P & K 37 K4
Kirkton Manor
    Border..................18 C2
Kirkton of Airlie
    Angus...................47 L6
Kirkton of
    Auchterhouse
    Angus...................48 B8
Kirkton of
    Barevan Highld ...65 K5
Kirkton of Collace
    P & K....................38 C2
Kirkton of
    Glenbuchat
    Abers....................57 J3
Kirkton of Logie
    Buchan Abers ...69 J7
Kirkton of
    Menmuir Angus ..48 E4
Kirkton of
    Monikie Angus ..48 E8
Kirkton of Rayne
    Abers....................68 D7
Kirkton of Skene
    Abers....................58 F4
Kirkton of
    Strathmartine
    Angus...................38 F1
Kirkton of Tealing
    Angus...................48 C8
Kirkton of Tough
    Abers....................58 C3
Kirktown Abers 69 J2
Kirktown Abers 69 K4
Kirktown of Alvah
    Abers....................68 D3
Kirktown of
    Bourtie Abers 58 F1
Kirktown of
    Fetteresso
    Abers....................58 F7
Kirktown of
    Mortlach Moray...67 H6
Kirktown of
    Slains Abers 69 K8
Kirkurd Border..........17 M1
Kirkwall Ork 86 c6
Kirkwall Airport
    Ork.......................86 c6
Kirk Yetholm
    Border..................20 C4
Kirn Ag & B 25 K3
Kirriemuir Angus......48 C5
Kirtlebridge D & G......9 M7
Kirtomy Highld 81 M3
Kirtonhill W Duns 26 D4
Kirwaugh D & G 3 J4
Kishorn Highld..........62 C6
Kittybrewster
    C Aber..................59 H4
Knaven Abers 69 G5
Knock Highld.............51 K4
Knock Moray.............67 L4
Knock W Isls 84 g2
Knockally Highld.......79 K3
Knockan Highld.........76 F6
Knockando Moray......66 F6
Knockbain Highld......64 E5
Knockbain Highld......64 E5
Knock Castle
    N Ayrs...................25 L5
Knockdee Highld.......83 H4
Knockdow Ag & B.....25 J4
Knockeen S Ayrs........7 G3

Knockenkelly
N Ayrs......**14** D4
Knockentiber
E Ayrs......**15** K2
Knockinlaw E Ayrs...**15** K2
Knocknain D & G......**2** B3
Knockrome Ag & B...**23** K4
Knocksheen D & G...**7** M5
Knockvennie
Smithy D & G......**8** D7
Knowe D & G......**7** G7
Knowehead D & G...**8** A4
Knoweside S Ayrs...**15** G6
Kyleakin Highld......**52** B1
Kyle of Lochalsh
Highld......**62** B8
Kylerhea Highld......**52** B2
Kylesku Highld......**76** F2
Kylesmorar Highld...**52** C6
Kyles Scalpay
W Isls......**84** e4
Kylestrome Highld...**76** F2

L

Lacasaigh W Isls...**84** f3
Lacasdal W Isls...**84** f2
Lady Ork......**86** d4
Ladybank Fife......**38** E5
Ladygill S Lans...**17** H4
Lag D & G......**8** F5
Laga Highld......**42** D4
Lagavulin Ag & B...**12** C1
Lagg N Ayrs......**14** B5
Laggan Highld......**53** L6
Laggan Highld......**54** F6
Lagganlia Highld...**55** K5
Laid Highld......**80** F4
Laide Highld......**71** L3
Laig Highld......**51** G7
Laigh Clunch
E Ayrs......**26** E8
Laigh Fenwick
E Ayrs......**15** L2
Laigh Glenmuir
E Ayrs......**16** C5
Laighstonehall
S Lans......**27** J7
Lairg Highld......**77** M7
Lambden Border......**19** L2
Lamberton Border...**31** K6
Lamington S Lans...**17** J3
Lamlash N Ayrs......**14** C3
Lanark S Lans......**17** G2
Landerberry Abers...**58** E4
Land-hallow
Highld......**79** L2
Langbank Rens......**26** D4
Langdyke Fife......**38** E6
Langholm D & G......**10** C5
Langlee Border......**19** H3
Langside P & K......**37** G5
Langwell House
Highld......**79** K4
Lanton Border......**19** J5
Laphroaig Ag & B...**12** C1
Larachbeg Highld...**42** E6
Larbert Falk......**28** B3
Largie Abers......**68** B7
Largiemore Ag & B...**24** F2
Largoward Fife......**39** H5
Largs N Ayrs......**25** L6
Largybeg N Ayrs...**14** D5
Largymore N Ayrs...**14** D4

Larkfield Inver......**25** L4
Larkhall S Lans......**27** K7
Lasswade Mdloth...**29** J5
Latheron Highld......**79** L2
Latheronwheel
Highld......**79** L3
Lathones Fife......**39** H5
Lauder Border......**30** C8
Laurencekirk
Abers......**49** H3
Laurieston D & G...**4** B3
Laurieston Falk......**28** B3
Law S Lans......**27** L7
Lawers P & K......**45** L7
Law Hill S Lans......**27** L7
Laxay W Isls......**84** f3
Laxdale W Isls......**84** f2
Laxford Bridge
Highld......**80** C6
Laxo Shet......**87** d4
Leachkin Highld......**64** F5
Leadburn Border...**29** H7
Leadhills S Lans......**17** G6
Lealt Highld......**61** H3
Lecht Gruinart
Ag & B......**22** E5
Leckbuie P & K......**45** L7
Leckmelm Highld...**72** F4
Ledaig Ag & B......**43** H8
Ledmore Junction
Highld......**76** F6
Leetown P & K......**38** C3
Legerwood Border...**19** J2
Leigh Knoweglass
S Lans......**27** H7
Leith C Edin......**29** H3
Leitholm Border...**20** B1
Lempitlaw Border...**20** B3
Lemreway W Isls...**84** f3
Lendalfoot S Ayrs...**6** D4
Lendrick Stirlg......**36** C6
Lendrum Terrace
Abers......**69** L6
Lenie Highld......**54** D1
Lennel Border......**20** C2
Lennox Plunton
D & G......**4** A5
Lennoxtown
E Duns......**27** H3
Lenzie E Duns......**27** H4
Leochel-Cushnie
Abers......**57** L4
Lephin Highld......**60** B4
Lerags Ag & B......**34** B3
Lerwick Shet......**87** d6
Leslie Abers......**58** B1
Leslie Fife......**38** D6
Lesmahagow
S Lans......**16** F2
Leswalt D & G......**2** B3
Letham Angus......**48** E6
Letham Border......**19** K7
Letham Falk......**28** B2
Letham Fife......**38** E4
Letham Grange
Angus......**49** G7
Lethendy P & K......**47** H7
Lethenty Abers......**58** B2
Lethenty Abers......**68** F6
Letterewe Highld...**71** L7
Letterfearn Highld...**52** D2
Letterfinlay
Lodge Hotel
Highld......**53** K6
Lettermorar
Highld......**51** M7

Letters Highld......**72** F4
Lettershaw S Lans...**17** H5
Lettoch Highld......**56** C2
Lettoch Highld......**66** D7
Leuchars Fife......**39** G3
Leumrabhagh
W Isls......**84** f3
Leurbost W Isls......**84** f3
Leven Fife......**38** F7
Levenwick Shet......**87** c7
Leverburgh W Isls...**84** d5
Lewiston Highld......**64** D8
Leylodge Abers......**58** E3
Leys Abers......**69** J4
Leys P & K......**47** K8
Leysmill Angus......**48** F6
Leys of Cossans
Angus......**48** C6
Lhanbryde Moray...**67** G3
Libberton S Lans...**17** J2
Liberton C Edin......**29** J4
Liddesdale
Highld......**42** F4
Liff Angus......**38** E2
Lilliesleaf Border...**19** H4
Limekilnburn
S Lans......**27** J7
Limekilns Fife......**28** E2
Limerigg Falk......**28** B4
Limmerhaugh
E Ayrs......**16** C4
Lincluden D & G......**9** G6
Lindores Fife......**38** D4
Linicro Highld......**70** B7
Linktown Fife......**29** J1
Linkwood Moray......**66** F3
Linlithgow W Loth...**28** D3
Linsidemore
Highld......**74** D2
Lintlaw Border......**31** H6
Lintmill Moray......**67** L2
Linton Border......**20** B4
Linwood Rens......**26** E5
Lionacleit W Isls...**85** b7
Lional W Isls......**84** g1
Lismore Ag & B......**43** G7
Little Airies D & G...**3** J5
Little Brechin
Angus......**48** F4
Littleburn Highld...**64** F4
Little Dunkeld
P & K......**47** G7
Little Knox D & G...**4** E3
Littlemill Abers......**57** H6
Littlemill Highld...**65** L4
Little Scatwell
Highld......**64** B3
Little Sypland
D & G......**4** C4
Littleton Angus......**48** B6
Littleton D & G......**4** B4
Liurbost W Isls......**84** f3
Livingston W Loth...**28** E5
Livingston Village
W Loth......**28** E5
Loan Falk......**28** C3
Loanhead Mdloth...**29** J5
Loaningfoot D & G...**5** G4
Loans S Ayrs......**15** J3
Lochailort Highld...**52** B8
Lochaline Highld...**42** D7
Lochans D & G......**2** C4
Locharbriggs
D & G......**9** H6
Lochavich Ag & B...**34** D4
Lochawe Ag & B...**35** G2

Loch Baghasdail
W Isls......**85** c8
Lochboisdale
W Isls......**85** c8
Lochbuie Ag & B...**33** J3
Lochcarron Highld...**62** D6
Lochdon Ag & B......**33** L2
Lochdonhead
Ag & B......**33** L2
Lochead Ag & B......**24** D3
Lochearnhead
Stirlg......**36** D3
Lochee C Dund......**38** F2
Locheilside
Station Highld......**43** K2
Lochend Highld......**64** F6
Lochfoot D & G......**8** F7
Lochgair Ag & B...**24** F1
Lochgelly Fife......**38** C8
Lochgilphead
Ag & B......**24** E2
Lochgoilhead
Ag & B......**35** H6
Lochieheads Fife...**38** D5
Lochill Moray......**67** G2
Lochindorb Lodge
Highld......**66** B7
Lochinver Highld...**76** D4
*Loch Lomond and
The Trossachs
National Park*......**36** A5
Lochluichart
Highld......**63** L2
Lochmaben D & G...**9** J5
Lochmaddy W Isls...**85** c6
Loch Maree Hotel
Highld......**71** L7
Loch nam
Madadh W Isls...**85** c6
Loch Ness Highld...**54** E1
Lochore Fife......**38** C7
Lochranza N Ayrs...**24** F7
Lochside Abers......**49** H4
Lochside D & G......**9** G6
Lochside Highld...**65** J4
Lochslin Highld......**75** J5
Lochton S Ayrs......**6** F6
Lochty Angus......**48** E4
Lochty Fife......**39** H5
Lochuisge Highld...**42** F5
Lochwinnoch
Rens......**26** C6
Lochwood D & G......**9** J3
Lockerbie D & G......**9** K5
Logan E Ayrs......**16** C5
Loganlea W Loth...**28** C6
Logie Angus......**49** H4
Logie Fife......**38** F4
Logie Moray......**66** C4
Logie Coldstone
Abers......**57** K4
Logie Newton
Abers......**68** C6
Logie Pert Angus...**49** G4
Logierait P & K......**46** F6
Logierieve Abers...**69** H8
Lonbain Highld......**61** L4
Londubh Highld......**71** K5
Lonemore Highld...**71** J6
Longforgan P & K...**38** E2
Longformacus
Border......**30** E6
Longhaven Abers...**69** L6

Longhope Ork...........86 b7
Longleys P & K...........47 L7
Longmanhill Abers...68 E2
Longmorn Moray 66 F3
Longnewton
　　Border...............19 J4
Long Newton
　　E Loth................30 B5
Longniddry E Loth...29 L3
Longridge W Loth....28 C5
Longriggend
　　N Lans................27 L4
Longside Abers.........69 K5
Longwood D & G.......4 C3
Longyester E Loth....30 C5
Lonmay Abers...........69 J3
Lonmore Highld........60 D5
Lootcherbrae
　　Abers................68 B4
Lornty P & K............47 J6
Lossiemouth
　　Moray................66 F1
Lothbeg Highld.......79 G6
Lothmore Highld......79 G6
Low Barbeth D & G...2 B2
Lower Breakish
　　Highld................51 L2
Lower Diabaig
　　Highld................62 C3
Lower Gledfield
　　Highld................74 D4
Lower Killeyan
　　Ag & B................12 A2
Lower Largo Fife......39 G6
Low
　　Gartachorrans
　　Stirlg................26 E2
Low Salchrie D & G...2 B2
Low Torry Fife.........28 D2
Loyal Lodge
　　Highld................81 J6
Lucklawhill Fife.......39 G3
Ludag W Isls............85 b9
Luffness E Loth.........30 B3
Lugar E Ayrs............16 C5
Luggate Burn
　　E Loth................30 D4
Luggiebank N Lans...27 K4
Lugton E Ayrs..........26 D7
Luib Highld..............61 J8
Luing Ag & B............33 L5
Lumloch E Duns.......27 H4
Lumphanan Abers ...58 B4
Lumphinnans Fife...38 C8
Lumsden Abers.........57 K2
Lunan Angus............49 H6
Lunanhead Angus...48 D6
Luncarty P & K.........38 A2
Lundie Angus...........38 E1
Lundin Links Fife....39 G6
Lundin Mill Fife.......39 G6
Lunga Ag & B............33 L5
Lunna Shet...............87 d4
Luss Ag & B..............35 L8
Lussagiven Ag & B ...23 L2
Lusta Highld.............60 D3
Luthermuir Abers...49 G3
Luthrie Fife..............38 E4
Lybster Highld.........83 J7
Lynchat Highld........55 J5
Lyne Border.............18 B2
Lyne of Skene
　　Abers................58 E4
Lyness Ork..............86 b7
Lyth Highld...............83 K3
Lythmore Highld.....82 F3

M

Macduff Abers..........68 D2
Macharioch Ag & B..13 J7
Machrie N Ayrs.........14 A3
Machrihanish
　　Ag & B................13 G5
Machrins Ag & B......32 E8
Macmerry E Loth......29 L4
Madderty P & K........37 K3
Maddiston Falk.........28 C3
Maggieknockater
　　Moray................67 H5
Maidens S Ayrs.........15 G7
Mail Shet...................87 d6
Mainland Ork............86 c6
Mainland Shet 87 c5
Mains of Balhall
　　Angus................48 E4
Mains of
　　Balnakettle
　　Abers................49 G2
Mains of Dalvey
　　Highld................66 D7
Mains of
　　Haulkerton
　　Abers................49 H2
Mains of Lesmoir
　　Abers................67 K8
Mains of
　　Melgunds
　　Angus................48 E5
Mainsriddle D & G ...5 G4
Maligar Highld..........61 G2
Mallaig Highld..........51 L6
Mallaigvaig Highld...51 L5
Malleny Mills
　　C Edin................29 G5
Manais W Isls............84 d5
Mandally Highld........53 L5
Manish W Isls............84 d5
Mannel Ag & B..........80 C7
Mannofield C Aber...59 H4
Manorhill Border.....19 K3
Mansfield E Ayrs......16 C6
March S Lans.............17 J6
Margnaheglish
　　N Ayrs................14 D3
Margrie D & G...........3 M5
Marionburgh
　　Abers................58 D4
Marishader Highld...61 H2
Marjoriebanks
　　D & G.................9 J5
Markinch Fife...........38 E6
Markle E Loth...........30 C3
Marwick Ork 86 b5
Marybank Highld.....64 D4
Maryburgh Highld....64 E3
Maryculter Abers....59 G5
Marygold Border......31 G6
Maryhill C Glas........27 G4
Maryhill
　　Crematorium
　　C Glas................27 G4
Marykirk Abers........49 H3
Marypark Moray......66 F6
Maryport D & G........2 D7
Maryton Angus........49 H5
Marywell Abers.......58 B6
Marywell Abers.......59 H5
Marywell Angus......49 G7
Masonhill
　　Crematorium
　　S Ayrs................15 J5

Mauchline E Ayrs......15 L4
Maud Abers...............69 H5
Mauld Highld............64 C6
Maxton Border.........19 J4
Maxwell Town
　　D & G.................9 G6
Maybole S Ayrs.........15 H7
Mayfield Mdloth.......29 K5
Mearns E Rens.........26 F7
Meigle P & K.............47 L7
Meikle Carco D & G..16 F6
Meikle Earnock
　　S Lans................27 J7
Meikle Kilmory
　　Ag & B................25 H6
Meikle Obney
　　P & K.................47 G8
Meikleour P & K........47 J7
Meikle Wartle
　　Abers................68 D7
Meldrum Stirlg.........36 F7
Melfort Ag & B..........34 B5
Mellon Charles
　　Highld................71 K3
Mellon Udrigle
　　Highld................71 K3
Melness Highld.........81 J3
Melrose Border........19 H3
Melsetter Ork..........86 b7
Melvaig Highld.........71 H4
Melvich Highld.........82 C3
Memsie Abers...........69 H2
Memus Angus............48 C5
Mennock D & G.........16 F7
Menstrie Clacks........37 H7
Meoble Highld...........52 C7
Merkadale Highld.....60 F7
Methil Fife................38 F7
Methilhill Fife..........38 F7
Methlick Abers.........69 G6
Methven P & K..........37 L3
Mey Highld................83 K2
Miabhig W Isls...........84 d2
Miavaig W Isls...........84 d2
Mid Ardlaw Abers....69 H2
Midbea Ork...............86 c4
Mid Beltie Abers......58 C5
Mid Calder W Loth...28 E5
Mid Clyth Highld......83 K7
Mid Culbeuchly
　　Abers................68 C3
Middlebie D & G........9 L6
Middlebridge
　　P & K.................46 D3
Middle Kames
　　Ag & B................24 F1
Middlethird
　　Border...............19 K2
Middleton Ag & B......40 B7
Middleton P & K.......38 B6
Middleton Park
　　C Aber................59 H3
Middleyard E Ayrs...15 M3
Midlem Border.........19 H4
Mid Mains Highld....64 B7
Midpark Ag & B........25 H6
Midtown Highld........81 J4
Mid Yell Shet............87 d3
Migvie Abers.............57 K4
Milesmark Fife.........28 E2
Millbreck Abers........69 J5
Millbuie Abers..........58 F4
Millbuie Highld.........64 E4
Millcraig Highld........74 E7
Millerhill Mdloth......29 J4
Millerston C Glas......27 H5

Millheugh S Lans......27 K7
Millhouse Ag & B.....25 G4
Millhousebridge
　　D & G.................9 K5
Milliken Park Rens ..26 D6
Mill of Drummond
　　P & K.................37 H4
Mill of Haldane
　　W Duns..............26 D2
Millport N Ayrs........25 K7
Milltimber C Aber....59 G5
Milltown Abers.........57 G4
Milltown Abers.........57 K3
Milltown D & G.........10 C6
Milltown of
　　Campfield
　　Abers................58 C5
Milltown of
　　Edinvillie** Moray...67 H6
Milltown of
　　Learney** Abers.....58 C5
Milnathort P & K.....38 B6
Milngavie E Duns....27 G4
Milovaig Highld.......60 B4
Milton D & G..............2 F4
Milton D & G..............8 E7
Milton Highld.............61 L5
Milton Highld.............64 D7
Milton Highld.............64 E4
Milton Highld.............75 G6
Milton Highld.............83 L5
Milton Inver..............26 C5
Milton Moray............56 F2
Milton Moray............67 L2
Milton P & K.............47 G4
Milton Stirlg.............36 B6
Milton W Duns.........26 D4
Milton Bridge
　　Mdloth................29 H5
Milton Morenish
　　P & K.................36 D1
Milton of
　　Auchinhove
　　Abers................58 B5
Milton of
　　Balgonie** Fife.....38 E7
Milton of
　　Buchanan** Stirlg ..26 E1
Milton of Campsie
　　E Duns................27 H3
Milton of Leys
　　Highld................65 G6
Milton of Murtle
　　C Aber................59 G5
Milton of Tullich
　　Abers................57 J6
Minard Ag & B...........34 D7
Mingarrypark
　　Highld................42 D3
Minishant S Ayrs.....15 J6
Minnigaff D & G.........3 J2
Minnonie Abers........68 E3
Mintlaw Abers..........69 J5
Minto Border............19 H5
Mireland Highld.......83 K4
Mitchellslacks
　　D & G.................9 G3
Mochrum D & G.........3 H5
Moffat D & G..............9 J2
Mol-chlach Highld...51 G3
Mollinsburn N Lans...27 J4
Mondynes Abers.......49 J1
Moneydie P & K........37 M2
Moniaive D & G.........8 D4
Monifieth Angus.......39 H2
Monikie Angus..........48 E8

Monimail Fife............38 E5
Monkton S Ayrs 15 J4
Monreith D & G............3 H6
Montgarrie Abers....58 B2
Montrose Angus......49 H5
Monymusk Abers....58 D3
Monzie P & K............37 H3
Moodiesburn
  N Lans......................27 J4
Moonzie Fife............38 E4
Morangie Highld......75 G5
Morar Highld............51 L6
Moray
  Crematorium
  Moray......................67 J3
Morebattle Border....20 B4
Morefield Highld......72 E3
Morenish P & K........36 D1
Morham E Loth........30 C4
Morningside
  C Edin......................29 H4
Morningside
  N Lans......................27 L7
Morphie Abers..........49 H4
Mortonhall
  Crematorium
  C Edin......................29 H5
Morvich Highld........52 E2
Moscow E Ayrs........15 L2
Moss Ag & B............40 B7
Mossat Abers............57 K2
Mossbank Shet........87 d4
Mossblown S Ayrs....15 K4
Mossburnford
  Border......................19 K6
Mossdale D & G..........8 B3
Mossdale E Ayrs..........7 K2
Mossend N Lans........27 K6
Mosspaul Hotel
  Border......................10 D3
Moss-side Highld......65 K4
Mosstodloch
  Moray......................67 H3
Mossyard D & G..........3 L5
Motherwell N Lans....27 K6
Moulin P & K............46 E4
Moultavie Highld......74 E7
Mountain Cross
  Border......................28 F8
Mountgerald
  House Highld......64 E3
Mount Lothian
  Mdloth 29 H6
Mouswald D & G........9 J7
Mowhaugh Border....20 B5
Moy Highld..............54 C8
Moy Highld..............65 J7
Moyle Highld............52 D2
Muasdale Ag & B......13 H2
Muchalls Abers........59 G6
Muck Highld............41 K1
Mugdock Stirlg........27 G3
Mugeary Highld........61 G6
Muirden Abers..........68 D4
Muirdrum Angus......48 F8
Muiresk Abers..........68 D5
Muirhead Angus......38 E1
Muirhead Fife..........38 E6
Muirhead N Lans......27 J4
Muirkirk E Ayrs........16 D4
Muirmill Stirlg..........27 J2
Muir of Fowlis
  Abers......................58 B3
Muir of
  Miltonduff
  Moray......................66 E3

Muir of Ord
  Highld......................64 E4
Muirshearlich
  Highld......................44 B1
Muirtack Abers..........69 J6
Muirton P & K............37 J5
Muirton Mains
  Highld......................64 C4
Muirton of
  Ardblair P & K......47 J7
Mulben Moray..........67 H4
Mull Ag & B..............33 J1
Munlochy Highld......65 G4
Munnoch N Ayrs......26 B8
Murkle Highld............83 H2
Murlaggan Highld....52 F6
Murroes Angus..........39 G1
Murthill Angus..........48 D5
Murthly P & K............47 H8
Musselburgh
  E Loth......................29 K4
Mutehill D & G............4 C5
Muthill P & K............37 H4
Mybster Highld........83 H5
Myrebird Abers........58 E5
Myredykes Border....11 G3

N

Naast Highld............71 J5
Na Buirgh W Isls......84 d4
Nairn Highld..............65 K3
Navidale House
  Hotel Highld........79 J5
Navity Highld............65 J2
Neap Shet..................87 d5
Nedd Highld..............76 D3
Neilston E Rens........26 E6
Nemphlar S Lans......17 G1
Nenthorn Border......19 K2
Nereabolls Ag & B....22 E7
Nerston S Lans..........27 H6
Nether Blainslie
  Border......................19 H2
Netherbrae Abers....68 F3
Netherburn
  S Lans......................27 L8
Nethercleuch
  D & G..........................9 K5
Nether Crimond
  Abers......................58 F2
Nether Dallachy
  Moray......................67 H2
Nether Fingland
  S Lans......................17 H7
Nether Handwick
  Angus......................48 B7
Nether
  Howcleugh
  S Lans......................17 K6
Nether Kinmundy
  Abers......................69 K5
Netherlaw D & G........4 C6
Netherley Abers......59 G6
Nethermill D & G........9 H5
Nethermuir Abers....69 G5
Netherplace
  E Rens......................26 F7
Netherton Angus......48 E5
Netherton N Lans......27 K7
Netherton P & K........47 J6
Netherton Stirlg......27 G3
Nethertown
  Highld......................83 L1
Netherurd Border......17 L1

Nether
  Whitecleuch
  S Lans......................17 G5
Nethy Bridge
  Highld......................56 B2
New Abbey D & G........5 G2
New Aberdour
  Abers......................69 G2
New Alyth P & K........47 K6
Newark Ork..............86 e4
Newarthill N Lans......27 K6
Newbattle Mdloth....29 J5
Newbie D & G..............5 L3
Newbigging
  Angus......................39 H1
Newbigging
  Angus......................47 L7
Newbigging
  Angus......................48 C8
Newbigging S Lans....17 K1
Newbridge C Edin....28 F4
Newbridge D & G........9 G6
Newburgh Abers......59 J1
Newburgh Abers......69 H3
Newburgh Fife..........38 D4
New Byth Abers........68 F4
Newcastleton
  Border......................10 E5
Newcraighall
  C Edin......................29 J4
New Cumnock
  E Ayrs......................16 C6
New Deer Abers........69 G5
New Elgin Moray......66 F3
Newfield Highld........75 H6
New Galloway
  D & G..........................8 B6
New Gilston Fife......39 G5
Newhaven C Edin....29 H3
Newhouse N Lans......27 L6
New Lanark S Lans....17 G2
New Lanark
  Village S Lans......17 G2
Newlandrig
  Mdloth....................29 K6
Newlands Border......10 E4
Newlands of
  Dundurcas
  Moray......................67 G4
New Langholm
  D & G........................10 C5
New Leeds Abers......69 J4
New Luce D & G............2 E3
Newmachar Abers....59 G2
Newmains N Lans......27 L6
Newmarket W Isls....84 f2
New Mill Abers..........58 E8
Newmill Border........19 G7
Newmill Moray..........67 K4
Newmill of
  Inshewan
  Angus......................48 C4
Newmills C Edin......29 G5
Newmills Fife............28 D2
Newmiln P & K..........38 B2
Newmilns E Ayrs......16 B2
New Pitsligo Abers....69 G3
Newport Highld........79 K4
Newport-on-Tay
  Fife..........................39 G2
New Prestwick
  S Ayrs......................15 J4
New Sauchie
  Clacks......................37 J7
Newseat Abers..........68 D7
Newstead Border......19 H3

New Stevenston
  N Lans......................27 K6
Newton Ag & B..........34 F7
Newton Border..........19 J5
Newton Highld..........64 F4
Newton Highld..........65 H5
Newton Highld..........65 J2
Newton Highld..........83 L5
Newton Mdloth........29 J4
Newton Moray..........66 E2
Newton Moray..........67 H2
Newton S Lans..........17 H3
Newton S Lans..........27 H6
Newton W Loth........28 E3
Newton Ferry
  W Isls......................84 c5
Newtongrange
  Mdloth....................29 J5
Newtonhill Abers....59 G6
Newtonloan
  Mdloth....................29 J5
Newton Mearns
  E Rens......................26 F7
Newtonmill Angus....48 F4
Newtonmore
  Highld......................55 H5
Newton of
  Balcanquhal
  P & K........................38 B5
Newton of
  Balcormo Fife......39 H6
Newton Stewart
  D & G..........................3 J3
Newton
  Wamphray
  D & G..........................9 K3
Newtown D & G..........16 F7
Newtown Highld......54 B4
Newtown of
  Beltrees Rens......26 D6
Newtown St
  Boswells
  Border......................19 J3
New Trows S Lans......16 F2
Newtyle Angus..........47 L7
New Winton
  E Loth......................29 L4
Newyork Ag & B........34 D5
Nigg C Aber..............59 H5
Nigg Highld..............75 H6
Nigg Ferry Highld....75 H7
Nisbet Border............19 K4
Nisbet Hill Border....31 G7
Nitshill C Glas..........26 F6
North
  Ballachulish
  Highld......................43 L4
North Berwick
  E Loth......................30 C2
North Connel
  Ag & B......................34 C1
North Duntulm
  Highld......................70 C6
North Erradale
  Highld......................71 H5
Northfield C Aber....59 G4
North Haven Shet....87 e7
North Kessock
  Highld......................65 G5
North Middleton
  Mdloth....................29 K6
North Millbrex
  Abers......................68 F5
North Milmain
  D & G..........................2 C4
Northmuir Angus....48 C5

North Queensferry
Fife 28 F3
North Ronaldsay
Ork 86 e3
North Ronaldsay
Airport Ork 86 e3
North Shian
Ag & B 43 H7
North Third Stirlg 27 K1
Northton W Isls 84 d5
North Uist W Isls 85 b6
Norwick Shet 87 e1
Norwood Clacks 37 J8
Nostie Highld 62 D8
Nybster Highld 83 L3

O

Oakbank W Loth 28 E5
Oakley Fife 28 D1
Oathlaw Angus 48 D5
Oban Ag & B 34 B2
Oban Airport
Ag & B 34 C1
Obney P & K 47 G8
Occumster Highld ...83 J7
Ochiltree E Ayrs 15 L5
Ockle Highld 42 B3
Old Aberdeen
C Aber 59 H4
Oldany Highld 76 D2
Old Auchenbrack
D & G 8 D3
Old Bridge of Urr
D & G 4 D2
Old Dailly S Ayrs 6 F3
Old Deer Abers 69 J5
Oldhamstocks
E Loth 30 F4
Old Inns Services
N Lans 27 K3
Old Kilpatrick
W Duns 26 E4
Oldmeldrum Abers ...68 F8
Old Rayne Abers 68 D8
Oldshoremore
Highld 80 C4
Old Struan P & K 46 C4
Old Wick Highld 83 L5
Olgrinmore Highld 83 G5
Ollaberry Shet 87 c3
Ollach Highld 61 H6
Olrig House Highld 83 H3
Onich Highld 43 K4
Opinan Highld 71 H6
Orbliston Moray 67 G3
Orbost Highld 60 D5
Ord Abers 68 C3
Ordhead Abers 58 C3
Ordie Abers 57 K5
Ordiequish Moray 67 H3
Orkney Islands Ork ...86 c6
Orkney Neolithic
Ork 86 b6
Ormiscaig Highld 71 K4
Ormiston E Loth 29 L4
Ormsaigmore
Highld 41 L4
Ormsary Ag & B 24 C4
Oronsay Ag & B 23 G2
Orphir Ork 86 b6
Orroland D & G 4 D5
Ose Highld 60 E6
Oskaig Highld 61 H6
Oskamull Ag & B 41 L7

Otter Ferry Ag & B ...24 F2
Otternish W Isls 84 c5
Otterswick Shet 87 d3
Our Dynamic
Earth C Edin 29 H4
Overscaig Hotel
Highld 77 J4
Overton C Aber 59 G3
Overtown N Lans 27 L7
Oxnam Border 19 L5
Oxton Border 30 B7
Oykel Bridge
Hotel Highld 73 K2
Oyne Abers 58 D1

P

Pabail W Isls 84 g2
Padanaram Angus ...48 C6
Paisley Rens 26 E5
Paisley Woodside
Crematorium
Rens 26 E5
Palmerston E Ayrs ...15 L5
Palnackie D & G 4 E4
Palnure D & G 3 J3
Panbride Angus 39 J1
Pannanich Wells
Hotel Abers 57 J6
Papa Westray
Airport Ork 86 c3
Papigoe Highld 83 L5
Papple E Loth 30 D4
Park D & G 8 F4
Parkgate D & G 9 H4
Parkgrove
Crematorium
Angus 48 F6
Parkhall W Duns 26 E4
Parkside N Lans 27 L6
Partick C Glas 26 F5
Pathhead Fife 38 E8
Pathhead Mdloth 29 K5
Path of Condie
P & K 37 M5
Patna E Ayrs 15 K7
Paxton Border 31 J7
Peathill Abers 69 H2
Peat Inn Fife 39 G5
Peebles Border 18 C2
Peinchorran
Highld 61 H7
Peinlich Highld 60 F3
Pencaitland E Loth ...29 L5
Penicuik Mdloth 29 H6
Penifiler Highld 61 G6
Peninver Ag & B 13 J4
Penkill S Ayrs 6 F3
Pennan Abers 68 F2
Pennycross Ag & B ...33 G3
Pennyghael
Ag & B 33 H3
Pennyglen S Ayrs 15 H7
Penpont D & G 8 E4
Penrioch N Ayrs 13 L1
Perceton N Ayrs 15 J2
Percyhorner Abers ...69 H2
Perth P & K 38 B3
Perth
Crematorium
P & K 38 A3
Peterculter C Aber 58 F5
Peterhead Abers 69 L5
Petterden Angus 48 C7
Pettinain S Lans 17 J2

Pettycur Fife 29 H2
Pettymuk Abers 59 G1
Philiphaugh
Border 18 F4
Philpstoun W Loth 28 E3
Phones Highld 55 G6
Pierowall Ork 86 C3
Pinminnoch
S Ayrs 6 E4
Pinmore S Ayrs 6 E4
Pinwherry S Ayrs 6 E5
Piperhill Highld 65 K4
Pirnie Border 19 K4
Pirnmill N Ayrs 13 L1
Pitagowan
P & K 46 C3
Pitblae Abers 69 J2
Pitcairngreen
P & K 37 M3
Pitcalnie Highld 75 H6
Pitcaple Abers 58 D1
Pitcarity Angus 48 B4
Pitchroy Moray 66 E6
Pitcox E Loth 30 E4
Pitfichie Abers 58 D3
Pitglassie Abers 68 D5
Pitgrudy Highld 75 H3
Pitlessie Fife 38 E5
Pitlochry P & K 46 E5
Pitmachie Abers 68 C8
Pitmain Highld 55 H5
Pitmedden Abers 69 G8
Pitmedden
Garden Abers 69 G8
Pitmuies Angus 48 F6
Pitmunie Abers 58 C3
Pitroddie P & K 38 C3
Pitscottie Fife 39 G5
Pittarrow Abers 49 H2
Pittenweem Fife 39 J6
Pitteuchar Fife 38 D7
Pittodrie House
Hotel Abers 58 D1
Pittulie Abers 69 H2
Plains N Lans 27 L5
Plean Stirlg 27 L2
Pleasance Fife 38 D5
Plockton Highld 62 C7
Polbain Highld 76 B6
Polbeth W Loth 28 D5
Polglass Highld 76 C6
Polgown D & G 8 C2
Polloch Highld 42 F3
Pollokshaws
C Glas 27 G6
Pollokshields
C Glas 27 G5
Polmont Falk 28 C3
Polnish Highld 52 B8
Poltalloch Ag & B ...34 B7
Polton Mdloth 29 J5
Polwarth Border 30 F7
Pomathorn
Mdloth 29 H6
Poolewe Highld 71 K5
Pool of Muckhart
Clacks 37 L7
Portachoillan
Ag & B 24 C6
Port-an-Eorna
Highld 62 B7
Port Appin Ag & B ...43 H7
Port Askaig Ag & B ...23 H5
Portavadie Ag & B ...24 F4
Port Bannatyne
Ag & B 25 J5

Port Charlotte
Ag & B 22 E6
Port Driseach
Ag & B 25 G4
Port Ellen Ag & B 12 C1
Port Elphinstone
Abers 58 E2
Portencalzie D & G ...6 B7
Portencross
N Ayrs 25 K8
Portessie Moray 67 K2
Port Glasgow
Inver 26 C4
Portgordon Moray 67 J2
Portgower Highld 79 H5
Port Henderson
Highld 71 H6
Portincaple Ag & B ..35 J8
Portinnisherrich
Ag & B 34 D5
Portknockie
Moray 67 K2
Portlethen Abers 59 H6
Portling D & G 4 F4
Port Logan D & G 2 D6
Portmahomack
Highld 75 K5
Port Mor Highld 41 K1
Portnacroish
Ag & B 43 H6
Portnaguran
W Isls 84 g2
Portnahaven
Ag & B 22 D7
Portnalong Highld 60 E7
Port nan Giuran
W Isls 84 g2
Port nan Long
W Isls 84 c5
Port Nis W Isls 84 g1
Portobello C Edin 29 J4
Port of Menteith
Stirlg 36 D6
Port of Ness W Isls ...84 g1
Portpatrick D & G 2 B4
Port Ramsay
Ag & B 43 H7
Portree Highld 61 G5
Portskerra Highld 82 C3
Portslogan D & G 2 B3
Portsonachan
Hotel Ag & B 34 F3
Portsoy Abers 68 B2
Portuairk Highld 41 K3
Port Wemyss
Ag & B 22 D7
Port William D & G 3 H6
Portyerrock D & G 3 K7
Posso Border 18 B3
Potarch Abers 58 B6
Potterton Abers 59 H3
Pouton D & G 3 K5
Powfoot D & G 5 K2
Powmill P & K 37 L7
Presnerb Angus 47 J3
Preston Border 31 G6
Prestonpans
E Loth 29 K4
Prestwick S Ayrs 15 J4
Prestwick Airport
S Ayrs 15 J4
Priestland E Ayrs 16 B2
Primrosehill
Border 31 G6
Primsidemill
Border 20 B4

Prora E Loth 30 C3
Protstonhill Abers...68 F2
Pumpherston
  W Loth...................28 E4

Q

Quarff Shet 87 c6
Quarrier's Village
  Inver...................26 C5
Quarrywood
  Moray..................66 E2
Quarter N Ayrs..........25 L6
Quarter S Lans 27 J7
Queen Elizabeth
  Forest Park
  Stirlg 36 B6
Queenslie C Glas 27 H5
Queenzieburn
  N Lans 27 J3
Quixwood Border ..31 G5
Quoig P & K 37 H3
Quothquan S Lans.....17 J2
Quoyburray Ork....86 c6
Quoyloo Ork............86 b5

R

Raasay Highld 61 J5
Rachan Mill Border ..17 L3
Racks D & G 9 H7
Rackwick Ork....86 a7
Raddery Highld......65 H3
Radernie Fife 39 G5
Rafford Moray 66 C3
Raigbeg Highld 65 J8
Rait P & K 38 D3
Ralia Highld 55 H5
Ramasaig Highld 60 B5
Ramscraigs Highld ..79 K3
Ranfurly Rens...........26 D5
Rankinston E Ayrs...15 L6
Rannoch Station
  P & K.................45 G5
Raploch Stirlg 37 G7
Rapness Ork...........86 c4
Rascarrel D & G........4 D5
Rashfield Ag & B......25 K2
Ratagan Highld.......52 E2
Rathen Abers 69 J3
Rathillet Fife.........38 F3
Ratho C Edin 28 F4
Ratho Station
  C Edin 28 F4
Rathven Moray......67 K2
Rattar Highld 83 J2
Rattray P & K.........47 J7
Ravenscraig
  N Lans 27 K6
Ravenstruther
  S Lans 17 H1
Rearquhar Highld....75 G3
Reay Highld 82 D3
Redburn Highld 65 L5
Redcastle D & G......4 E2
Redcastle Highld ...64 E4
Redding Falk..........28 C3
Reddingmuirhead
  Falk..................28 C3
Redford Abers 49 J3
Redford Angus......48 F7
Redfordgreen
  Border.................18 E6
Redgorton P & K...38 A2

Redhill Abers...........58 E4
Redland Ork...........86 b5
Redmyre Abers.......49 J2
Redpath Border........19 J3
Redpoint Highld......71 H7
Redstone P & K.......38 C1
Reiff Highld 76 B5
Reisque Abers........59 G2
Reiss Highld...........83 L5
Relugas Moray........66 B5
Renfrew Rens.........26 F5
Renton W Duns.......26 D3
Resaurie Highld.....65 H5
Resipole Highld......42 E4
Resolis Highld........65 G2
Rest and be
  thankful Ag & B..35 J6
Reston Border.........31 H6
Reswallie Angus.....48 E6
Rheindown Highld...64 D5
Rhicarn Highld........76 D4
Rhiconich Highld....80 C5
Rhicullen Highld....74 F6
Rhireavach Highld ..72 D3
Rhives Highld........75 H2
Rhonehouse D & G...4 C3
Rhu Ag & B 26 B2
Rhubodach Ag & B..25 H4
Rhunahaorine
  Ag & B 24 C8
Rhynd P & K 38 B4
Rhynie Abers...........67 L8
Rhynie Highld.........75 J5
Riccarton Border......10 F3
Riccarton E Ayrs 15 K3
Riddell Border.........19 H4
Rigg D & G 10 B8
Riggend N Lans.......27 K4
Righoul Highld.......65 K4
Rigside S Lans 17 G3
Ringford D & G 4 C4
Ringorm Moray........67 G5
Risabus Ag & B........12 B2
Riverford Highld......64 E4
Roadmeetings
  S Lans 28 B7
Roadside E Ayrs.......16 B5
Roadside Highld 83 H4
Roag Highld...........60 D5
Roan of Craigoch
  S Ayrs..................7 G2
Roberton Border......18 F6
Roberton S Lans 17 H4
Robgill Tower
  D & G 9 M7
Rockcliffe D & G.......4 E4
Rockfield Highld......75 K5
Rockville Ag & B......25 L1
Rodel W Isls 84 d5
Rogart Highld 78 C7
Roghadal W Isls.......84 d5
Romanno Bridge
  Border.................29 G8
Romesdal Highld....60 F4
Rona Highld 61 K3
Ronachan Ag & B....24 C7
Rora Abers..............69 K4
Rosarie Moray........67 J4
Rosebank S Lans......27 L7
Rosehall Highld.......77 K7
Rosehearty Abers ...69 H2
Roseisle Moray........66 E2
Rosemarkie Highld ..65 H3
Rosemount P & K....47 J7
Rosewell Mdloth......29 J6
Roskhill Highld........60 D5

Roslin Mdloth..........29 H5
Rosneath Ag & B 26 B2
Ross D & G 4 B6
Rossland Rens.........26 E4
Roster Highld..........83 J7
Rosyth Fife.............28 F2
Rothes Moray..........67 G4
Rothesay Ag & B 25 J5
Rothiebrisbane
  Abers.................68 E6
Rothiemay Moray ...67 M5
Rothiemurchus
  Lodge Highld 56 B4
Rothiemurchus
  Visitor Centre
  Highld................55 L3
Rothienorman
  Abers.................68 D7
Rothmaise Abers....68 D7
Rottal Lodge
  Angus.................48 B3
Roucan D & G...........9 H6
Roucan Loch
  Crematorium
  D & G 9 H6
Roughpark Abers....57 H3
Roundyhill Angus...48 C6
Rousay Ork............86 c4
Routenburn
  N Ayrs................25 L6
Rowanburn D & G....10 D6
Rowardennan
  Stirlg 35 L7
Roxburgh Border......19 L4
Royal Yacht
  Britannia
  C Edin................29 H3
Roy Bridge
  Highld................44 D1
Ruaig Ag & B 40 D6
Rubha Ban W Isls....85 c9
Ruecastle Border.....19 J5
Rùm Highld............50 F5
Rumbach Moray ...67 J4
Rumbling Bridge
  P & K..................37 L7
Rumford Falk..........28 C3
Runtaleave Angus ...47 L3
Ruskie Stirlg 36 D7
Rutherford Border....19 K4
Rutherglen S Lans....27 H6
Ruthrieston
  C Aber................59 H4
Ruthven Abers........67 L5
Ruthven Angus.......47 L6
Ruthven Highld.......55 H5
Ruthwell D & G 5 J2

S

Saddell Ag & B........13 K3
St Abbs Border.........31 J5
St Agnes Border.......30 E5
St Andrews Fife.......39 H4
St Andrews
  Botanic
  Garden Fife........39 H4
St Ann's D & G 9 J4
St Boswells Border...19 J3
St Catherines
  Ag & B 35 G6
St Colmac Ag & B....25 H5
St Combs Abers.......69 K2
St Cyrus Abers 49 J4
St David's P & K.......37 K4

St Fergus Abers........69 K4
St Fillans P & K.........36 F3
St John's Kirk
  S Lans 17 J3
St John's Town of
  Dalry D & G...........8 B6
St Katherines
  Abers.................68 E7
St Madoes P & K 38 C3
St Margaret's
  Hope Ork............86 c7
St Martin's P & K......38 B2
St Mary's Ork 86 c6
St Monans Fife 39 H6
St Ninians Stirlg 37 G8
St Quivox S Ayrs......15 J5
St Vigeans Angus.....49 G7
Salen Ag & B............42 C7
Salen Highld 42 D4
Saline Fife...............37 L8
Salsburgh
  N Lans 27 L5
Saltburn Highld 75 G7
Saltcoats N Ayrs......15 G2
Samsonlane Ork......86 d5
Samuelston E Loth..30 B4
Sanaigmore
  Ag & B 22 E4
Sandaig Highld 51 L5
Sandavore Highld ...51 G7
Sanday Ork.............86 d4
Sanday Airport Ork..86 d4
Sandbank Ag & B 25 K3
Sandend Abers........68 B2
Sandford S Lans.......16 E2
Sandhaven Abers....69 H2
Sandhead D & G 2 D5
Sandhole Ag & B......34 E7
Sandness Shet........87 b5
Sandwick Shet.........87 c7
Sandwick W Isls.......84 g2
Sandyford D & G 9 L4
Sandyhills D & G 4 F4
Sangobeg Highld.....80 F3
Sangomore Highld...80 F3
Sanna Bay Highld ...41 K3
Sanndabhaig
  W Isls.................84 g2
Sannox N Ayrs.........14 C1
Sanquhar D & G 16 F7
Sarclet Highld 83 L6
Sauchen Abers........58 D3
Saucher P & K 38 C2
Sauchieburn Abers ..49 G3
Scalasaig Ag & B.....32 E8
Scalloway Shet........87 c6
Scalpay Highld........61 J7
Scamodale Highld ..43 G2
Scaniport Highld 64 F6
Scarba Ag & B 33 K6
Scarfskerry Highld...83 J2
Scarinish Ag & B 40 D7
Scatsta Airport
  Shet...................87 c4
Scone P & K 38 B3
Sconser Highld........61 H7
Scoonie Fife............38 F6
Scoraig Highld........72 C3
Scotlandwell
  P & K..................38 C6
Scotscalder
  Station Highld......83 G4
Scotsmill Abers.......58 B2
Scotstoun C Glas......26 F5
Scottish Seabird
  Centre E Loth........30 C2

Scottish Wool
   Centre Stirlg......36 C7
Scourie Highld 80 B6
Scourie More
   Highld.................80 B6
Scousburgh Shet 87 c7
Scrabster Highld.....83 G2
Scraesburgh
   Border 19 K5
Scullomie Highld 81 J4
Seafield Highld 61 G5
Seafield W Loth 28 D5
Seafield
   Crematorium
   C Edin...................29 J4
Seamill N Ayrs.........25 L8
Selkirk Border 19 G4
Sellafirth Shet..........87 d2
Seton Mains
   E Loth...................29 L4
Sgiogarstaigh
   W Isls....................84 g1
Shader W Isls...........84 f1
Shandford Angus......48 D4
Shandon Ag & B 26 B2
Shandwick Highld....75 J6
Shapinsay Ork..........86 c5
Shawbost W Isls 84 e2
Shawhead D & G 8 F6
Shawsburn S Lans....27 K7
Shearington D & G 5 H2
Shebster Highld.......82 E3
Sheddens E Rens......27 G6
Sheigra Highld 80 B4
Shennanton D & G 3 H3
Shenval Moray..........66 F7
Shetland Islands
   Shet......................87 c5
Shettleston C Glas....27 H5
Shiel Bridge Highld ..52 E2
Shieldaig Highld 62 C4
Shieldhill D & G 9 H5
Shieldhill Falk..........28 B3
Shieldhill House
   Hotel S Lans.........17 J2
Shields N Lans..........27 K7
Shielfoot Highld 42 D3
Shielhill Angus.........48 C5
Shielhill Inver 25 L4
Shillford E Rens........26 E6
Shinness Highld 77 L5
Shirvan Ag & B..........24 E2
Shiskine N Ayrs........14 B4
Shortlees E Ayrs.......15 K3
Shotts N Lans...........28 B6
Shougle Moray..........66 F4
Shuna Ag & B 33 M5
Shurrery Highld........82 F4
Shurrery Lodge
   Highld...................82 F4
Siabost W Isls...........84 e2
Siadar W Isls.............84 f1
Sibster Highld...........83 K5
Silverburn Mdloth....29 G6
Silverford Abers........68 E2
Simprim Border.........20 C1
Sinclair's Hill
   Border 31 G7
Sinclairston E Ayrs...15 L6
Sinnarhard Abers......57 K3
Skaill Ork..................86 d6
Skara Brae Ork 86 b5
Skares E Ayrs............16 B6
Skateraw Abers........59 G6
Skateraw E Loth.......30 F4
Skeabost Highld 60 F5

Skelbo Highld............75 H3
Skelbo Street
   Highld...................75 H3
Skelmorlie N Ayrs.....25 L5
Skelpick Highld.........81 L4
Skelston D & G 8 E5
Skene House
   Abers....................58 E4
Skerray Highld..........81 K3
Skerricha Highld........80 C5
Skiall Highld..............82 E3
Skigersta W Isls........84 g1
Skinflats Falk...........28 B2
Skinidin Highld..........60 C5
Skipness Ag & B........24 F6
Skipper's Bridge
   D & G....................10 C5
Skirling Border..........17 L2
Skirza Highld.............83 L2
Skulamus Highld.......51 K2
Skye of Curr
   Highld...................56 B1
Slacks of
   Cairnbanno
   Abers....................68 F5
Slamannan Falk........28 B4
Sleasdairidh
   Highld...................74 E3
Slickly Highld.............83 K3
Sliddery N Ayrs.........14 B5
Sligachan Highld 61 G7
Sligrachan Ag & B 25 K1
Slockavullin
   Ag & B 34 B7
Slumbay Highld 62 D6
Smailholm Border......19 K3
Smearisary Highld.....42 D2
Smerral Highld...........79 L2
Smithstown
   Highld...................71 J4
Smithton Highld........65 H5
Smoo Highld..............80 F3
Snade D & G 8 E5
Soay Highld................51 G3
Solas W Isls..............84 c5
Solwaybank D & G.....10 B6
Sorbie D & G 3 J5
Sordale Highld...........83 G3
Sorisdale Ag & B.......41 H4
Sorn E Ayrs................16 B4
Sortat Highld.............83 K3
Sound Muir
   Moray....................67 H4
South Alloa Falk 37 J8
South
   Ballachulish
   Highld...................43 K5
Southend Ag & B........13 H7
Southerness D & G.....5 G4
South Erradale
   Highld...................71 H7
Southfield Falk..........27 L4
South Gyle C Edin.....29 G4
South Kessock
   Highld...................65 G5
South Lanarkshire
   Crematorium
   S Lans...................27 J7
Southmuir Angus.....48 C5
South
   Queensferry
   C Edin...................28 F3
South Ronaldsay
   Ork.......................86 c7
South Shian
   Ag & B 43 H7

South Tarbrax
   S Lans 28 D7
South Uist W Isls.....85 c8
Spean Bridge
   Highld...................53 K8
Spey Bay Moray.......67 H2
Speybridge Highld 56 C1
Speyview Moray........67 G6
Spinningdale
   Highld...................74 F4
Spittal E Loth 30 B3
Spittal Highld............83 H5
Spittalfield P & K......47 H7
Spittal of
   Glenmuick
   Abers....................57 G7
Spittal of
   Glenshee P & K 47 H3
Spittal-on-Rule
   Border 19 J5
Spott E Loth 30 E4
Spottiswoode
   Border 30 D7
Springburn C Glas 27 G5
Springfield D & G.......10 B7
Springfield Fife 38 E5
Springholm D & G 8 E7
Springside N Ayrs.....15 J2
Sprouston Border 20 A3
Stadhlaigearraidh
   W Isls....................85 b7
Staffin Highld............70 D7
Stair E Ayrs...............15 K5
Stairhaven D & G........2 E4
Stand N Lans.............27 K5
Standburn Falk.........28 C4
Stane N Lans.............28 B6
Stanhope Border.......17 L4
Stanley P & K.............38 B2
Staoinebrig W Isls....85 b8
Star Fife...................38 E6
Staxigoe Highld.........83 L5
Steelend Fife.............37 L8
Steele Road
   Border 10 F4
Stein Highld...............60 D3
Stenhouse D & G 8 D4
Stenhousemuir
   Falk......................28 B2
Stenscholl Highld......70 D7
Stenton E Loth..........30 D4
Steornabhagh
   W Isls....................84 f2
Stepford D & G 8 E5
Stepps N Lans...........27 H5
Stevenston N Ayrs....15 H2
Stewartfield
   S Lans 27 H7
Stewarton E Ayrs.....15 K1
Stichill Border...........19 L2
Stilligarry W Isls........85 b7
Stirling Abers............69 L6
Stirling Stirlg............37 G8
Stirling Castle
   Stirlg....................37 G8
Stirling Services
   Stirlg....................27 L2
Stobo Border.............18 B2
Stobs Castle
   Border 19 G7
Stockbriggs S Lans...16 F3
Stoer Highld..............76 C3
Stonefield Castle
   Hotel Ag & B 24 E4
Stonehaven Abers.....59 G7
Stonehouse S Lans...27 K8

Stonewells Moray 67 G2
Stoneybridge
   W Isls....................85 b8
Stoneyburn
   W Loth..................28 D5
Stoneykirk D & G........2 C4
Stoneywood
   C Aber...................59 G3
Stoneywood Falk......37 L2
Stornoway W Isls......84 f2
Stornoway Airport
   W Isls....................84 g2
Stotfield Moray.........66 F1
Stove Shet................87 c7
Stow Border 19 G1
Straanruie Highld......56 B3
Strachan Abers.........58 D6
Strachur Ag & B.........34 F6
Straiton Mdloth.........29 H5
Straiton S Ayrs............7 H2
Straloch Abers...........59 G2
Straloch P & K............47 G4
Stranraer D & G 2 C3
Strath Highld..............71 J5
Strathan Highld.........76 D4
Strathan Highld.........81 J3
Strathaven S Lans.....16 D1
Strathblane Stirlg......27 G3
Strathcanaird
   Highld...................72 F2
Strathcarron
   Highld...................62 E6
Strathcoil Ag & B.......33 K2
Strathdon Abers.........57 H3
Strathkinness Fife.....39 G4
Strathloanhead
   W Loth..................28 C4
Strathmashie
   House Highld.........54 F6
Strathmiglo Fife........38 C5
Strathpeffer
   Highld...................64 D3
Strathtay P & K..........46 E5
Strathwhillan
   N Ayrs..................14 D3
Strathy Highld............82 B3
Strathy Inn Highld.....82 B3
Strathyre Stirlg..........36 C4
Strelitz P & K.............38 C1
Strichen Abers...........69 H4
Stroma Highld............83 L1
Stromeferry
   Highld...................62 D7
Stromness Ork..........86 b6
Stronachlachar
   Stirlg....................35 L5
Stronafian Ag & B 25 H3
Stronchrubie
   Highld...................76 F5
Strone Ag & B 25 L3
Strone Highld.............44 B1
Strone Highld.............64 E8
Stronenaba Highld.....53 J3
Stronmilchan
   Ag & B 35 G2
Stronsay Ork.............86 d5
Stronsay Airport
   Ork.......................86 d5
Strontian Highld........43 G4
Struan Highld.............60 E6
Struan P & K..............46 C4
Strutherhill S Lans.....27 K7
Struthers Fife............38 F5
Struy Highld...............64 B6
Stuartfield Abers........69 H5
Stynie Moray..............67 H3

Succoth Ag & B........35 K6
Suisnish Highld........51 J3
Sullom Shet............87 C4
Sullom Voe Shet....87 C4
Sumburgh Airport
  Shet..................87 c8
Sundaywell D & G 8 E5
Sunderland Ag & B....22 E5
Sundhope Border.....18 E4
Sunnylaw Stirlg......37 G7
Swiney Highld.........79 M2
Swinton Border.......31 H8
Swordale Highld.....64 E2
Swordland Highld....52 B6
Swordly Highld.......81 M3
Symbister Shet.......87 d4
Symington S Ayrs....15 J3
Symington S Lans....17 J3
Syre Highld............81 L6

T

Tain Highld.............75 G5
Tain Highld.............83 J3
Tairbeart W Isls......84 e4
Talisker Highld.......60 E7
Talladale Highld......71 L7
Talla Linnfoots
  Border..................17 M5
Tallaminnock S Ayrs....7 J3
Talmine Highld........81 J3
Tangusdale W Isls....85 b9
Tankerness Ork.......86 c6
Tannach Highld.......83 K6
Tannachie Abers......58 E8
Tannadice Angus....48 D5
Tannochside
  N Lans..................27 J6
Taobh Tuath W Isls....84 d5
Tarbert Ag & B........24 B7
Tarbert Ag & B........24 E5
Tarbert W Isls.........84 e4
Tarbet Ag & B.........35 K6
Tarbet Highld.........52 B6
Tarbet Highld.........80 B5
Tarbolton S Ayrs.....15 K4
Tarbrax S Lans........28 D7
Tarfside Angus........48 D1
Tarland Abers..........57 K4
Tarskavaig Highld....51 J4
Tarves Abers..........69 G7
Tauchers Moray......67 J4
Taychreggan
  Hotel Ag & B.........34 F3
Tay Forest Park
  P & K...................46 C4
Tayinloan Ag & B....13 H1
Taynuilt Ag & B.......34 E2
Tayport Fife...........39 G2
Tayvallich Ag & B....24 C2
Tealing Angus.........48 C8
Teangue Highld......51 K4
Teanord Highld.......64 F2
Teindside Border....18 F7
Tempar P & K..........45 L5
Templand D & G........9 J5
Temple Mdloth.......29 J6
Temple of Fiddes
  Abers...................49 K1
Terregles D & G........9 G6
Teviothead Border....10 D2
Thainstone Abers....58 E2
Thankerton S Lans....17 J2
The Braes Highld....61 H7
The Brunt E Loth.....30 E4

The Den N Ayrs.......26 C7
The Linn
  Crematorium
  E Rens.................27 G6
The Lochs Moray.....67 G2
The Murray S Lans....27 H7
The Neuk Abers.......58 D5
The Ross P & K.........37 G3
Thirlestane Border...30 C8
Thomastown
  Abers...................68 B6
Thornhill D & G.........8 F3
Thornhill Stirlg.......36 E7
Thornliebank
  E Rens.................26 F6
Thornton Angus......48 C6
Thornton Fife.........38 E7
Thorntonhall
  S Lans..................27 G7
Thorntonloch
  E Loth..................30 F4
Thornydykes
  Border..................30 D8
Threave S Ayrs........15 J7
Three Miletown
  W Loth.................28 E3
Throsk Stirlg...........28 B1
Throughgate
  D & G....................8 F5
Thrumster Highld....83 L6
Thurso Highld.........83 G2
Tibbermore P & K....37 L3
Tibbers D & G...........8 E3
Tibbie Shiels Inn
  Border..................18 C5
Tigerton Angus.......48 E4
Tigh a Ghearraidh
  W Isls..................85 b6
Tigharry W Isls........85 b6
Tighnabruaich
  Ag & B.................25 G4
Tillicoultry Clacks....37 J7
Tillietudlem S Lans....28 F1
Tillybirloch Abers....58 D4
Tillyfourie Abers......58 C3
Tillygreig Abers.......59 G2
Tillyrie P & K...........38 B6
Timpanheck D & G...10 B7
Timsgarry W Isls.....84 d2
Timsgearraidh
  W Isls..................84 d2
Tingwall Airport
  Shet....................87 c6
Tingwell Ork...........86 c5
Tinwald D & G...........9 H5
Tiree Ag & B...........40 D7
Tiree Airport
  Ag & B.................40 C7
Tiretigan Ag & B......24 C6
Tiroran Ag & B.........33 G2
Toab Shet..............87 c8
Tobermory Ag & B...41 L5
Toberonochy
  Ag & B.................33 L5
Tobha Mor W Isls....85 b7
Tocher Abers..........68 D7
Tochieneal Moray....67 L2
Todhills Angus........48 C8
Toft Shet................87 c3
Tokavaig Highld......51 J3
Tolastadh W Isls.....84 g2
Tolsta W Isls...........84 g2
Tomatin Highld.......65 J8
Tomchrasky Highld....53 K3
Tomdoun Highld.....53 H5
Tomich Highld.........63 L8

Tomich Highld.........64 E5
Tomich Highld.........74 F7
Tomich Highld.........78 A7
Tomintoul Moray....56 E2
Tomnacross
  Highld..................64 D6
Tomnavoulin
  Moray..................56 F1
Tongland D & G.........4 C4
Tongue Highld........81 J4
Torbeg N Ayrs.........14 A4
Torboll Highld.........75 G2
Torbreck Highld......65 G6
Torcastle Highld......44 B2
Tore Highld.............64 F4
Torinturk Ag & B......24 D5
Tormore N Ayrs.......13 M3
Tornagrain Highld....65 J4
Tornaveen Abers......58 C4
Torness Highld........64 E8
Torphichen W Loth...28 C4
Torphins Abers........58 C5
Torquhan Border.....29 L8
Torran Highld..........61 J5
Torrance E Duns......27 H4
Torranyard N Ayrs...15 J1
Torridon Highld.......62 D3
Torridon House
  Highld..................62 D3
Torrin Highld...........51 J2
Torrisdale Ag & B....13 K3
Torrisdale Highld.....81 K3
Torrish Highld.........79 G5
Torrobull Highld......78 A7
Torry C Aber............59 H4
Torryburn Fife........28 D2
Torthorwald D & G.....9 H6
Torvaig Highld.........61 H5
Torwood Falk..........27 L2
Torwoodlee
  Border..................19 G2
Toscaig Highld........61 L6
Totaig Highld..........60 C4
Tote Highld.............60 F5
Tote Highld.............61 H3
Totronald Ag & B....40 F5
Totscore Highld......60 F2
Toulvaddie Highld....75 J5
Toward Ag & B........25 K5
Toward Quay
  Ag & B.................25 J5
Towie Abers............57 K3
Townend W Duns....26 D3
Townhead D & G.......9 H4
Townhead of
  Greenlaw D & G.....4 C3
Townhill Fife...........28 F1
Town Yetholm
  Border..................20 B4
Trabboch E Ayrs......15 K5
Trabbochburn
  E Ayrs..................15 L5
Tradespark Highld....65 K3
Tranent E Loth........29 L4
Trantelbeg Highld....82 C5
Trantlemore
  Highld..................82 C5
Traprain E Loth.......30 D4
Traquair Border.......18 E3
Treaslane Highld......60 F4
Treshnish Isles
  Ag & B.................41 G7
Tressait P & K..........46 C4
Tresta Shet.............87 c5
Tresta Shet.............87 e3
Trinafour P & K........46 B4

Trinity Angus..........48 F4
Trinity Gask P & K....37 K4
Trislaig Highld.........43 L2
Trochry P & K..........46 F7
Troon S Ayrs...........15 H3
Trossachs Stirlg......36 B5
Trossachs Pier
  Stirlg...................36 B6
Trumpan Highld......60 C3
Tullibody Clacks......37 H7
Tullich Highld..........64 F8
Tullich Highld..........75 J6
Tulliemet P & K........46 F5
Tulloch Abers..........68 F7
Tullochgorm Ag & B....34 D7
Tulloch Station
  Highld..................44 F1
Tullymurdoch
  P & K...................47 J5
Tullynessle Abers.....58 B2
Tummel Bridge
  P & K...................46 B5
Tundergarth D & G....9 L6
Turnberry S Ayrs.......6 E2
Turnhouse C Edin....29 G4
Turriff Abers...........68 D4
Tushielaw Inn
  Border..................18 D5
Twatt Ork...............86 b5
Twatt Shet..............87 c5
Twechar E Duns......27 J3
Tweedbank
  Border..................19 H3
Tweedsmuir
  Border..................17 L4
Twynholm D & G.......4 B4
Tyndrum Stirlg........35 K2
Tyninghame
  E Loth..................30 D3
Tynron D & G............8 E4

U

Uddingston S Lans...27 J6
Uddington S Lans....17 G3
Udny Green Abers....59 G1
Udny Station
  Abers...................59 G1
Ugadale Ag & B........13 K4
Uibhist A Deas
  W Isls..................85 c8
Uibhist A Tuath
  W Isls..................85 b6
Uig Ag & B...............40 F5
Uig Highld...............60 C4
Uig Highld...............60 F2
Uig W Isls...............84 d2
Uigshader Highld....61 G5
Uisken Ag & B.........32 E4
Ulbster Highld.........83 K7
Ullapool Highld.......72 E3
Ullinish Lodge
  Hotel Highld........60 E6
Ulsta Shet..............87 d3
Ulva Ag & B.............41 K7
Ulzieside D & G.......16 F7
Unapool Highld.......76 F2
Under
  Burnmouth
  Border..................10 E5
Unst Shet...............87 d1
Uphall W Loth.........28 E4
Uplawmoor E Rens...26 E7
Upper Ardchronie
  Highld..................74 E4

Upper Bighouse
Highld..................82 C4
Upper Breakish
Highld..................51 L2
Upper Dallachy
Moray 67 H2
Upper Dounreay
Highld..................82 E3
Upper Drumbane
Stirlg 36 E6
Upper Eathie
Highld..................65 J2
Upperglen Highld.....60 E4
Upper
Kinchrackine
Ag & B 35 G2
Upper Largo Fife 39 G6
Upper Lochton
Abers 58 D6
Upper Lybster
Highld..................83 J7
Upper Mulben
Moray 67 H4
Upper Ruscoe
D & G 3 L3
Upper Skelmorlie
N Ayrs..................25 L5
Uppertown Highld..83 L1
Upper Victoria
Angus....................39 J1
Upsettlington
Border 20 C1
Urquhart Moray..........67 G2
Urquhart Castle
Highld..................64 E8
Urray Highld..............64 D4
Usan Angus 49 H5
Uyeasound Shet......87 d2

V

Valtos Highld..............61 H2
Valtos W Isls 84 d2
Vatsetter Shet 87 d3
Vatten Highld..............60 D5
Veensgarth
Shet........................87 c6
Vidlin Shet 87 d4
Viewfield Moray 67 G2
Viewpark N Lans.....27 J6
Voe Shet 87 c4

W

Walbutt D & G............4 D2
Walkerburn Border...18 E3
Walkerton Fife 38 D6
Wallacetown
S Ayrs....................7 G2

Wallacetown
S Ayrs....................15 J5
Walls Shet................87 b5
Wallyford E Loth 29 K4
Walston S Lans..........17 K1
Wanlockhead D & G..17 G6
Warrenhill S Lans......17 J2
Warriston C Edin 29 H4
Warriston
Crematorium
C Edin 29 H3
Wasbister Ork............86 c4
Waterbeck D & G......9 M6
Waterfoot E Rens.....27 G7
Waterheads Border..29 H7
Waterloo Highld........51 K2
Waterloo N Lans.......27 L7
Waterloo P & K 47 G8
Waterside E Ayrs......15 K7
Waterside E Ayrs 15 L2
Waterside E Duns......27 J4
Waterstein Highld......60 B5
Watten Highld............83 J5
Wattston N Lans.......27 K4
Waulkmill Abers......58 C6
Wedderlairs Abers....68 F7
Weem P & K 46 D6
Weisdale Shet............87 c5
Wellbank Angus 48 D8
Welltree P & K..........37 K3
Wellwood Fife 28 E2
Wemyss Bay Inver....25 L4
West Barns E Loth....30 E3
West Cairngaan
D & G 2 D8
West Calder W Loth..28 D5
West Dunnet
Highld..................83 J2
Wester
Aberchalder
Highld..................54 E2
Westerdale Highld ...83 G5
Western Isles
W Isls 84 d5
Wester Ochiltree
W Loth..................28 D4
Wester Pitkierie
Fife 39 J6
Wester Ross
Highld..................72 C5
Westerton of
Rossie Angus.....49 G5
Westerwick Shet......87 c6
Westfield Highld........82 F3
Westfield N Lans.......27 J4
Westfield W Loth......28 C4
Westfields of
Rattray P & K......47 J6
West Haven Angus...39 J1
West Helmsdale
Highld..................79 H5

Westhill Abers..........58 F4
West
Huntingtower
P & K....................37 M3
West Kilbride
N Ayrs..................25 L8
West Linton
Border 28 F7
West Morriston
Border 19 J2
Westmuir Angus......48 B5
West Park Abers......58 E5
Westquarter Falk......28 B3
Westray Ork..............86 c3
Westray Airport
Ork........................86 c3
Westrigg W Loth......28 B5
Westruther Border..30 D7
West Saltoun
E Loth....................30 B5
West Sandwick
Shet......................87 d3
West Tarbert
Ag & B 24 E5
West Wemyss Fife ..38 E7
Weydale Highld........83 H3
Whaligoe Highld........83 K7
Whalsay Shet............87 d4
Whauphill D & G........3 J5
Whigstreet Angus....48 D7
Whinnie Liggate
D & G 4 C4
Whinnyfold Abers....69 K7
Whistlefield
Ag & B 35 J8
Whistlefield Inn
Ag & B 35 G8
Whitburn W Loth......28 C5
Whitchester
Border 30 F6
Whitebridge
Highld..................54 D3
Whitecairns Abers....59 H2
Whitecraig E Loth....29 K4
Whitecrook D & G......2 E4
Whitecross Falk........28 C3
Whiteface Highld......74 F4
Whitefarland
N Ayrs..................13 L2
Whitefaulds S Ayrs...15 H7
Whiteford Abers 58 D1
Whitehall Ork............86 d5
Whitehills Abers......68 C2
Whitehouse Abers....58 C3
Whitehouse Ag & B..24 D6
Whitekirk E Loth......30 D3
Whitemire Moray 66 B4
Whiteness Shet........87 c6
Whiterashes Abers..58 F2
Whiterow Highld......83 L5
Whiterow Moray......66 C3

Whitfield C Dund......39 G2
Whithorn D & G..........3 J6
Whiting Bay
N Ayrs..................14 D4
Whitlaw Border 19 G6
Whitletts S Ayrs......15 J5
Whitsome Border....31 H7
Wick Highld..............83 L5
Wick John o'
Groats Airport
Highld..................83 L5
Wigtown D & G..........3 J4
Wildmanbridge
S Lans 27 L7
Wilkhaven Highld....75 K4
Wilkieston W Loth....28 F5
Wilsontown S Lans...28 C7
Wilton Dean
Border 19 G6
Winchburgh
W Loth..................28 E4
Windhill Highld 64 E5
Windsole Abers 68 B3
Windygates Fife......38 E7
Winless Highld........83 K5
Wishaw N Lans 27 L7
Wiston S Lans 17 J3
Wolfclyde S Lans 17 K3
Wolfhill P & K 38 B2
Woodend Highld 42 F4
Woodend W Loth 28 C4
Woodhead Abers 68 E6
Woodhouselee
Mdloth 29 H5
Woodhouselees
D & G 10 D6
Woodland Abers......59 G2
Woodland S Ayrs......6 E3
Woodlands Abers....58 E6
Woodside Fife 39 G5
Woodside P & K......47 K8
Woolfords S Lans....28 D6
Wormit Fife..............38 F3

Y

Yarrow Border..........18 E4
Yarrow Feus
Border 18 E4
Yarrowford
Border 18 F4
Yell Shet..................87 d3
Yesnaby Ork............86 b5
Yetts o'Muckhart
Clacks 37 L6
Yieldshields S Lans ..28 B7
Yoker C Glas 26 F5
Ythanbank Abers....69 G7
Ythanwells Abers....68 C6
Ythsie Abers............69 G7